Identity Texts
the Collaborative Creation of Power
in Multilingual Schools

Identity Texts
the Collaborative Creation of Power
in Multilingual Schools

edited by
Jim Cummins and Margaret Early

IOEPress

A Trentham Book
Institute of Education Press, London

Institute of Education Press
20 Bedford Way
London
WC1H 0AL

First published 2011

British Library Cataloguing-in-Publication Data
A catalogue record for this book is available from the British Library

Page 24, 33: Copyright 2001 by J. Cummins. Reprinted with permission.

Page 29: Diagram copyright Vasilia Kourtis-Kazoullis. Reprinted with permission.

ISBN 978-1-85856-478-4

Designed and typeset by Trentham Books Ltd, Chester and printed by CPI Group (UK) Ltd, Croydon, CR0 4YY

Dedication

This book is dedicated to Patricia Chow who created the Dual Language Showcase at Thornwood public school in the Peel District Board of Education near Toronto. Many of the case studies in the book owe their initial inspiration to the Dual Language Showcase. Students' dual language stories can be viewed at http://thornwoodps.dyndns.org/dual/index.htm

The book is also dedicated to all teachers who work tirelessly in the interest of educational equity and social justice for marginalised students through transformative multiliteracies pedagogies, in particular those teachers from whom we have both learned so much.

Contents

Acknowledgements

We gratefully acknowledge the support of the Social Sciences and Humanities Research Council of Canada (SSHRC) in the funding of our national project, *From Literacy to Multiliteracies: Designing Learning Environments for Knowledge Generation within the New Economy*, and a second grant, with the Vancouver School Board, Investigating Alternative Accountability. Many of the cases and vignettes in this book are drawn from these projects and we owe a significant debt to all those with whom we worked closely and collaboratively during that time. Projects reported in the book were also supported by Canadian federal government funds associated with the Canada Research Chair awarded to Dr. Jim Cummins. We are also indebted to Anne White, Secretary in the Department of Language and Literacy Education at UBC, for keen insights and overall contributions to manuscript preparation. Our gratitude is also extended to Dr. Gillian Klein at Trentham Books for her patience, attention to detail and support throughout the process of writing this book.

Authors' biographical statements

Madiha Bajwa was born in Rubwa, Pakistan. She immigrated to Canada when she was in grade 7. She is currently studying in the Seneca College/York University General Arts program.

Vicki Bismilla is the Vice-President Academic and Chief Learning Officer at Centennial College in Toronto. Her area of interest is in exploring the role played by mother tongues in college students' acquisition of English.

Angeles Clemente is a full time professor and Chair of the Critical Applied Linguistics Research Group at the Language School of Benito Juárez Autonomous University of Oaxaca. She holds a PhD in Applied Linguistics from the University of London, where she was a Research Fellow during 2000-2001. She is a member of the Mexican Researchers' System (SNI) and conducts research in the area of sociolinguistics in the context of Mexico.

Sarah Cohen is an assistant professor in the Department of Literacy Education at Northern Illinois University. Her research focuses on the development of bilingualism and biliteracy in emergent bilingual students and on collaborating with teachers to promote multilingual teaching practices.

Jim Cummins is a Canada Research Chair in the Department of Curriculum, Teaching and Learning of OISE/University of Toronto. His research focuses on literacy development in multilingual school contexts as well as on the potential roles of technology in promoting language and literacy development.

Margaret Early is an associate professor in the Department of Language and Literacy Education at the University of British Columbia. Her research focuses on the development of multilingual/multimodal academic literacies in mainstream classrooms.

Nancy Dykstra teaches in an elementary school in Kitchener, Ontario, Canada. She has taught in English-medium and French-medium settings and through her practice she has found herself drawn to her English Language Learner (ELL) students. She is particularly interested in exploring how classroom teachers can better meet the academic and social needs of their ELL students.

Eithne Gallagher is an ESL teacher in the Elementary department of Marymount International School in Rome. Her writings on ESL and Mother-tongue have been published in several books and journals. She is the author of *Equal Rights to the Curriculum: Many Languages, One Message* (2008).

Frances Giampapa is a Lecturer in Education (TESOL/Applied Linguistics) at the Graduate School of Education, University of Bristol. Her research focuses on the politics of identity across multilingual contexts. In particular her work focuses on EAL students' L1 identity practices and literacies and the ways in which these are harnessed for the development of school literacies.

Mario López-Gopar is a professor in the Faculty of Languages of Benito Juárez Autonomous University of Oaxaca. He holds a doctorate in Second Language Education from the Ontario Institute for Studies in Education at the University of Toronto (OISE/UT). His PhD thesis was awarded both the 2009 AERA Second Language Research Dissertation Award and the 2009 OISE Outstanding Thesis of the Year Award. López-Gopar's main research interest is intercultural and multilingual education of Indigenous peoples in Mexico.

Sulmana Hanif was born in Karachi, Pakistan. She immigrated to Canada when she was in grade 4. She is currently enrolled at Humber College in Toronto studying Engineering.

Amanda Hennessey is a student at the University of Ottawa majoring in Second Language Teaching. She is presently working as a university language instructor and is interested in multicultural education and the impact of identity texts in second language classrooms. E-mail: ahenn100@uottawa.ca

Michael Higgins is an anthropologist who has been doing ethnographic research in the city of Oaxaca for more than 40 years. He is Professor Emeritus of Anthropology from the University of Northern Colorado. With Angeles Clemente he is the co-author of *Performing English with a Postcolonial Accent: Ethnographic Narratives from Mexico* (2008).

Kanta Khalid was born in Gujrawala, near Lahore in Pakistan and immigrated to Canada when she was in grade 4. She is currently enrolled at Centennial College in Toronto, working towards completing the Practical Nursing program. After college, Kanta plans to study Registered Nursing and to become a Nurse Practitioner and work in a hospital.

Vasilia Kourtis-Kazoullis is an assistant professor at the Department of Primary Education, University of the Aegean (Rhodes, Greece). Her research focuses on bilingualism and learning in electronic environments.

Donald Kissinger has an MA in TEFL/TESL from San Francisco State University and has taught in Cairo, San Francisco and Oaxaca. He is about to retire from full-time teaching in the BA TEFL program at Benito Juárez Autonomous University of

Oaxaca. His main research interests have been self-access language learning, phonology and morphology, but through involvement in the prison project, he has developed an additional interest in multilingualism and identity.

Jonathan Lambert is a classroom teacher in the English Department at Sichuan University for Nationalities, also known as Khampa University, in China. His present research includes language learning and teaching in multilingual environments.

Lisa Leoni works as a vice-principal for the York Region District School Board. She holds a Masters in Education from the Ontario Institute for Studies in Education at the University of Toronto. Her areas of interest encompass issues of identity, language, and the power of multicultural education to help students understand and appreciate the global society.

Dolors Masats is a researcher and teacher trainer in the Department of Language and Literature Education at the Universitat Autònoma de Barcelona. Her research focuses on conversational analysis for second language acquisition in multilingual school settings as well as on the benefits of video-making projects for media education, language awareness and teacher development.

Kimberly Meredith is a PhD student in the Language and Literacy Education department at the University of British Columbia specialising in Teaching English as a Second Language. Her research focuses on language and identity, multilingualism, dance, and critical pedagogy. She is particularly interested in how students make sense of their linguistic, kinesthetic, digital and multimodal semiotic resources within the differential (dis)empowering and privileging discourses of language education.

Rania Mirza is a teacher with the York Region District School Board in Ontario. She is currently completing her Masters in Education at the University of Toronto with a focus on Second Language Education. Her research focuses on practical approaches to affirming identities in multilingual classrooms, language learning among minority groups, and bilingual education.

Bonny Norton is Professor and Distinguished University Scholar in the Department of Language and Literacy Education, University of British Columbia, Canada. Her research addresses identity, language learning, critical literacy, and international development. Her website can be found at http://lerc.educ.ubc.ca/fac/ norton/

Nico Paluzzi is a student at the University of Ottawa, majoring in Second Language Teaching and working as a language instructor at the University of Ottawa. His interests include the role of multiliteracies in the language learning classroom. E-mail: npalu032@uottawa.ca.

Diane Potts is a Sessional Instructor in the Department of Language and Literacy Education at the University of British Columbia. Her research interests focus on knowledge mobilisation, the semiotic demands of working across multilingual, multimodal texts, and pedagogies which support students in engaging in these practices.

Gail Prasad is a doctoral student in Second Language Education at the Ontario Institute for Studies in Education (OISE). Gail has worked as a language and literacy teacher with students from Kindergarten through high school. Her research interests include students' plurilingual development and teachers' inclusive literacy practices in both English and French-language schools.

Tomer Shahar was born in Israel and was raised in an agricultural community. He immigrated to Canada when he was in grade 6. He will graduate from high school in 2011 and hopes to pursue a career in education and/or health sciences.

Perminder Sandhu is an elementary school teacher in the York Region District School Board, near Toronto.

Padma Sastri is a Teacher-Librarian with Peel District School Board and has worked with her Board on issues of equity and social justice over a number of years.

Jérémie Séror is an assistant professor at the Official Languages and Bilingualism Institute at the University of Ottawa. His research focuses on development of advanced academic literacies, second language writing and the language socialisation of multilingual students into educational institutions, disciplines and professions. E-mail: jseror@uottawa.ca

Kristin Snoddon is a Social Sciences and Humanities Research Council of Canada Postdoctoral Fellow with the School of Early Childhood Education, Ryerson University in Toronto. Her work focuses on early bilingual education in American Sign Language and English, and multiliteracies and language learning in young Deaf children.

Saskia Stille is a PhD candidate in the Department of Curriculum, Teaching, and Learning of the Ontario Institute for Studies in Education at the University of Toronto. Her research focuses on literacy development and she works with students and teachers to integrate knowledge media and information and communication technologies in teaching and learning activities.

William Sughrua is currently completing a PhD in applied linguistics from Canterbury Christ Church University in the UK. For many years, he has been a member of the faculty of the Language School of Benito Juárez Autonomous University of Oaxaca. His research interests are in critical applied linguistics, reflexive ethnography, and alternative academic writing.

Virginia Unamuno is senior researcher of the Consejo Nacional de Investigaciones Científicas at the Universidad de Buenos Aires (Argentina.) Her main research focuses on sociolinguistics and on education in multilingual contexts as well as on empowerment for language minority teachers.

A Note on Terminology

A wide variety of terms have been used to refer to students whose home language differs from the dominant language of the society, which is typically the primary language of instruction in schools. These terms differ across geographical contexts and over time within geographical contexts. The various terms are also loaded with ideological connotations and these have been hotly debated in the academic literature. For example, some scholars in the United States have objected to the term 'minority language students' because it appears to devalue the status of these students in comparison to 'majority language students'. Other scholars (eg Tove Skutnabb-Kangas [2000] in the European context) have defended the use of the term 'minority' because of the legal rights that certain minority groups have gained within educational and other social spheres. Terms commonly used in official policies to refer to students such as 'English-as-a-second-language' (ESL), English-as-an-additional-language (EAL), and 'English language learners' (ELL) are all seen as somewhat problematic by many scholars because they define students by what they lack, namely adequate proficiency in English to achieve academically without additional instructional support. To counter this, some scholars have used terms such as 'bilingual' or 'emergent bilingual' (eg Ofelia Garcia [2008] in the United States) to highlight the linguistic accomplishments of students rather than their presumed linguistic limitations.

The terms that focus on students' linguistic status intersect with terminology used to refer to students from social groups that have experienced long-standing or recent discrimination in the society. Terms such as 'minoritised', 'subordinated', 'oppressed', 'marginalised', 'racialised', and more recently from the Council of Europe, 'vulnerable', have been used to refer to the fact that students who experience academic underachievement frequently belong to social groups that have been subject to institutionalised racism or have been on the receiving end of what, in this volume, we call coercive relations of power.

We have decided to reflect the shifting identity locations of students and their communities by employing a variety of terms. The terms we use here, and those used in the broader research and policy literature, carry different nuances of meaning. Like identities, meanings are not static. By employing a variety of terms we remind the reader (and ourselves) that student identities shift in multiple ways according to the interactions students experience and the messages they receive in classrooms, schools and other social contexts. Thus terms such as 'bilingual' and 'emergent bilingual' highlight students' linguistic potential (not always realised because of the rapid loss of home languages in many contexts), as against the relatively neutral 'culturally and linguistically diverse', and sometimes we reflect common teacher and policy-maker usage such as ELL or EAL. Similarly, we employ a variety of terms to refer to the ways students and communities are positioned by the operation of societal power structures, while noting that not all bilingual/EAL students are marginalised or subordinated. Some are, in fact, in highly privileged situations (eg those in private international schools).

Throughout the book, we emphasise that educators have considerable power to affect student identity construction in positive (and, unfortunately, in negative) ways. Teachers' instructional choices within the classroom play a huge role in determining the extent to which students will emerge from an identity cocoon defined by their assumed limitations (eg the 'ESL student') to an interpersonal space defined by their talents and accomplishments, both linguistic and intellectual. For this to happen, teachers must 'see through' the institutional labels to the potential within. Our conscious strategy is therefore to trouble essentialised notions of student, teacher and community identities by emphasising that students and teachers alike are in a 'becoming' mode and the interactions they experience shape this process of becoming.

PART ONE
IDENTITY TEXTS

1

Introduction

Jim Cummins, Margaret Early

What is an 'identity text'?

We first used the term *identity text* to capture essential features of the work produced by students in the context of our project *From Literacy to Multiliteracies: Designing Learning Environments for Knowledge Generation within the New Economy.* The project ran from 2002 to 2006 and involved collaborative research with teachers primarily in the Vancouver and Toronto areas. The research explored the instructional spaces that opened up when the definition of 'literacy' was expanded beyond its traditional focus on linear print-based reading and writing skills in the dominant language. Specifically, we asked what pedagogical options become available to teachers when literacy is conceived as 'multiple', referring both to the 'new literacies' ushered in by rapid technological changes and the multilingual literacies practised by increasing numbers of people in linguistically diverse communities.

Identity texts described the products of students' creative work or performances carried out within the pedagogical space orchestrated by the classroom teacher. Students invest their identities in the creation of these texts – which can be written, spoken, signed, visual, musical, dramatic, or combinations in multimodal form. The identity text then holds a mirror up to students in which their identities are reflected back in a positive light. When students share identity texts with multiple audiences (peers, teachers, parents, grandparents, sister classes, the media, etc) they are likely to receive positive feedback and affirmation of self in interaction with these audiences. Although not always an essential component, technology acts as an amplifier to enhance the process of identity text production and dissemination.

In the Multiliteracies Project, we found evidence that the creation of dual language identity texts by bilingual students made a significant impact on both students' self-image and the quality of their learning. Specifically, as documented in Chapter 3, identity text creation:

- encouraged students to connect new information and skills to their background knowledge
- enabled students to produce more accomplished literacy work in the school language
- increased their awareness of the specialised language of school subject areas
- affirmed students' identities as intelligent, imaginative and linguistically talented
- increased their awareness of the relationships between their home language (L1) and the school language (L2)

We argue that identity texts represent a powerful pedagogical tool to promote equity for students from marginalised social backgrounds. Marginalisation can derive from discrimination based on a variety of factors – socioeconomic background, racialised status, linguistic, cultural or religious difference. Classroom interactions that enable students to create identity texts which showcase their intellectual, linguistic, multimodal, and artistic talents, challenge the devaluation of identity that many linguistically diverse and other marginalised students experience in contexts where their home languages or varieties of language are not explicitly acknowledged as intellectual and cultural resources. Creation of identity texts also helps students to develop knowledge of particular subject matter and engages them actively in literacy and cultural production or performance, at a cognitively appropriate level, at a time when their English language academic skills may still be far below the expectations for particular age or grade levels.

In short, the creation of identity texts represents a powerful tool in enabling marginalised students to develop 'identities of competence' (Manyak, 2004) in academic contexts. Identity text creation is one component of a broader pedagogical approach that articulates a 'counter-discourse' to the implicit devaluation of students' abilities, languages, cultures, and identities that occurs in classrooms where students' preferred ways of meaning making and home languages are ignored or treated with 'benign neglect'. Thus, the significance of identity texts within the broader context of pedagogy for marginalised students derives from their role as tools of empowerment, which we define as the collaborative creation of power (see Chapter 2).

In the next section, we briefly review how other authors have independently employed the term 'identity text' and related constructs. We limit our discussion to the construct of identity text although we are aware that there is a vast literature that addresses intersections between identity and literacy. Detailed discussion of that literature is beyond the scope of this book; we refer interested readers to key sources such as Gee (2004), Gérin-Lajoie, (2003), Holland *et al* (1998), McKinney and Norton, (2008), Moje and Luke (2009), Norton (2000, 2010, in press), and Pavlenko and Blackledge (2004).

Identity texts in previous studies

The term 'identity text' initially entered our academic lexicon in 2004 in the collaboration between Jim Cummins and Eleni Skourtou and Vasilia Kourtis-Kazoullis of the University of the Aegean in Rhodes, Greece. Vasilia's dissertation (Kourtis-Kazoullis, 2001) had focused on documenting the outcomes of a sister class project in which students from the Greek islands of Rhodes and Kassos carried out several joint projects with students from Toronto in Canada. The collaboration evoked a high level of engagement among the students in Greece. They initiated critical inquiry into a variety of issues (eg the Elgin/Parthenon marbles), carried out creative writing projects in both Greek and English, and explored local history and oral narratives from their communities (Skourtou, Kourtis-Kazoullis, and Cummins, 2006). The identity investment on the part of these students, which Vasilia documented in her dissertation, paralleled what we were observing in the Canadian context in the Dual Language Showcase (Chow and Cummins, 2003; Cummins, Chow, and Schecter, 2006) and Multiliteracies projects (Chapter 3). We subsequently introduced the term in a number of articles and attempted to link it to broader pedagogical frameworks (Cummins, 2004, 2006; Skourtou, Kourtis-Kazoullis and Cummins, 2006).

In recent years, the term has also been used by other authors. The first use that we noted was in an article by Pippa Stein and Denise Newfeld, who documented the implementation of multimodal pedagogical approaches in South African classrooms. Stein and Newfeld (2003) describe several pedagogical innovations that challenge the primacy of dominant notions of school-based literacy by opening up the space for multimodal ways of making meaning. They point out that 'the narrow focus in schooling on particular literacies favour those who enter the school system with rich semiotic resources in those domains' (2003:2842). They aimed to:

> draw attention to texts and communicative practices of teenagers who enter the school system with resources recruited from the multiple milieux of which

they are part, in their everyday lives. These hybrid urban texts challenge the existing boundaries of curricula which attempt to teach 'pure' language systems and 'pure' genres of texts. Our project has been thus to begin a process of recovery, of reclaiming the classroom as a transformatory space which has the potential to enable students' processes of becoming as fully expressive human beings within the context of a liberated South Africa. (2003:2842)

Stein and Newfeld refer to 'identity texts' in the context of a Body Tracing project in which students worked in pairs to make life size self-portraits. They assert that these 'powerful visual identity texts ... illuminate the distinctive ways in which, in the practices of making, identities are discovered, imagined, recognised and named' (p2846-2847). They describe the transformation among adolescent students in Robert Maungedzo's classroom in Soweto that resulted from the pedagogical changes he instituted that enabled his students to engage in cultural production. Students who were disengaged and failing in the context of a curriculum irrelevant to their experiences and aspirations became academically engaged and successful in response to projects which grounded literacy production in the realities of their own lives. The multi-modal projects the students carried out 'combined cloth-making, map-making, praise poems in indigenous languages and contemporary poems in English' (p2843). What motivated the students was the desire to speak and be heard. This is illustrated in the comment of one participant: 'I think this is the most precious thing I have ever done in my life. Since I began schooling I have never had an opportunity to discover my talents and gifts ... It's like I was fortified in knowledge and understanding' (Stein and Newfeld, 2003:2844).

Although they do not use the term 'identity text', Jennifer Rowsell and Kate Pahl (2007) elaborate a similar notion in discussing 'sedimented identities in texts'. They describe text making 'as a process involving the sedimentation of identities into the text, which then can be seen as an artefact that reflects, through its materiality, the previous identities of the meaning maker' (2007: 388). The metaphor of sedimentation evokes the slow process through which multiple grains of sand become assembled over time into rock. In the same way, every finished text reflects the experiential history or the layered identities of the text producer. Rowsell and Pahl outline the implications for pedagogy as follows:

Classrooms are spaces that can be infused with our students' identities. As children come to write, the host of experiences they have had since birth are brought to bear on the writing processes. By recognising and honoring that experience, teachers can bring students' identities into the classroom. Ways in

> which cultural patterns are handed down over time can be traced in children's texts. (2007:402)

Wohlwend (2009) draws on Rowsell and Pahl's (2007) notion of 'sedimented identities in text' in an article entitled 'Damsels in Discourse: Girls Consuming and Producing Identity Texts through Disney Princess Play'. She suggests that commercially produced toys are artefacts with anticipated identities. In other words, they incorporate 'identities that have been projected for consumers and that are sedimented by manufacturers' design practices and distribution processes' (p.59). She reported that when female kindergarten students played with Disney Princess dolls during writing workshop, they animated identities sedimented into toys and texts.

Although they did not use the term 'identity texts', Early and Gunderson (1993) made a plea nearly two decades ago for what they called 'authentic literacy' texts and practices. The principles underlying the production of these texts share many features with those articulated above. Early and Gunderson pointed out that definitions of literacy vary according to 'the social and cultural contexts of literacy in the community and in the home' (1993:102). They argued that these 'home grown' conceptions of literacy must be honoured in the classroom, and advocated that teachers and students *collaboratively* design pedagogical spaces that 'build on the considerable linguistic, social and cultural resources that children brought from their home/community' (1993:100). These authors make the case that for this to occur fundamental changes in the social relations between teachers and students are required, wherein teachers become learners of the different cultural histories, modes of representation, languages and discourses of the students in their classrooms, and 'students play an active role and exercise some control of their own reading, writing and learning' (1993:104). Implicit in such pedagogical practices is the affirmation of students' identities as highly able individuals, with agency in their own learning and something of value to offer.

Early and Gunderson reported on the design of 'enabling literacy environments' that expanded literacy beyond its traditional focus on linear print-based skills in the dominant language. Of specific interest is the work that Vancouver teachers and students engaged in to conduct ethnographies of what has now come to be known as the 'linguistic landscape' of their home communities. Tasks included studying the local communities, preparing and conducting surveys, interviewing residents, writing histories, drawing maps, taking photographs, making slide presentations and involving community members, including parents, as co-investigators. This work was conducted in both the L1 and the L2. Arguably, the products of these literacy practices were early examples of 'identity texts', intended 'to promote respect among children and between home and school communities' (1993:109).

The rationale and implementation of identity text work in classrooms has been most fully elaborated in *Authors in the Classroom* by Alma Flor Ada and Isabel Campoy (2004). Ada and Campoy stress the power of authorship to transform the lives of students, teachers and parents and contribute to building a more socially conscious and responsive society. They document the process whereby teachers, parents and children can create books that explore student and community experiences and realities, starting from simple prompts such as 'I am...' or 'Where I come from...'. Their book is a treasure trove of inspirational ideas for linking literacy, authorship, and identity. They point out that their pedagogical approach 'is designed to connect students' personal lives and identities with literacy' (2004:40). Although they don't explicitly use the term 'identity texts', their book covers the same pedagogical ground and they view authorship in the classroom as a transformative educational process (see Chapter 2 for elaboration on transformative pedagogy). In the Multiliteracies Project, we purchased multiple copies of *Authors in the Classroom* for teachers, as a catalyst for collaborative exploration of the power of authorship.

This power was documented in a quantitative research study carried out by Judith Bernhard and colleagues in the Miami area (Bernhard, Winsler, and Bleiker, 2004). Conducted during the 2003-2004 school year, the Early Authors Program (EAP) was a large-scale, early literacy program that involved 32 child care centres, 800 families and more than 1,000 children. The books were based on family histories and the children's interests and experiences. Parents, family members, caregivers, and 57 educators also wrote books. A total of 3,286 books, many of them dual language, were produced in English, Spanish, and Haitian-Creole.

The EAP was based on the principles articulated by Ada and Campoy (2004) in *Authors in the Classroom*. The EAP established a family literacy project at each preschool, and invited children, teachers, and parents to jointly write, illustrate and publish books. Each centre was equipped with computers, cameras, printers and a laminator to facilitate production of the books. The goal was to encourage children to learn to read and write from not only commercially published books but from their own very personal literature. Literacy specialists provided support to the teachers who were implementing the EAP in their classrooms.

The evaluation of the EAP used a pre-test/post-test experimental design and random selection of children within both the experimental and the control group. The EAP group consisted of 280 children selected at random from the consenting children in the 32 EAP classrooms, and 87 control children who were randomly selected from consenting families in non-EAP classrooms at similar centres, serving the same population in the same neighbourhoods. Findings on a wide variety of measures showed significantly stronger growth in language and literacy among the EAP children in comparison to the control children. There was also evidence of increased self-esteem. Bernhard *et al* (2006:2399) explain the outcomes as follows:

> The dramatic increase in EAP children's scores can be explained, we suggest, by focusing on the essential elements of the program. The children's experiences as early authors allowed them to see themselves in their self-made books and to talk about their own lives and interests. This identity investment resulted in increased pride, both in themselves and in their families.

Our notion of identity texts in the present volume is similar to the pedagogical initiatives described by Ada and Campoy (2004) and Stein and Newfeld (2003). Building on the reality that identities are infused or sedimented into literacy practices, we explore how identity text production can be harnessed by teachers as an instructional tool to promote literacy engagement and achievement among marginalised students. The work we describe complements a vigorous research effort in the UK during the past decade (and earlier) that has documented children's experience in multilingual environments and highlighted the multiple ways in which their home languages serve as cognitive and personal resources for learning (eg Conteh, Martin, and Robertson, 2007; Creese and Blackledge, 2010; Edwards, 1998; Issa and Williams, 2009; Kenner, 2000; Sneddon, 2009).

Recent initiatives in Canada have expanded the pedagogical landscape in imaginative ways. Marshall and Toohey (2010), for example, document how Grade 4 and Grade 5 students in Vancouver who came primarily from Punjabi-speaking home backgrounds used MP3 players to record stories of their grandparents' childhood experiences in India and then used these stories as the basis for the creation of dual language texts. Although the students engaged in a great deal of composing, editing, illustrating and translating, the project was seen by parents, students and the school as a whole as being 'something special' outside of the mainstream of schooling. Marshall and Toohey emphasise the importance of critical pedagogy as a means of going beyond just lip service to children's and their families' lives and experiences.

They argue that dialogue among teachers, students, and community members about the broader social and ethical issues (e.g., conflict, moral choices, etc.) embedded in the family stories is crucial in mobilising these narratives for powerful educational purposes.

At York University in Toronto, Lotherington (eg Lotherington and Chow, 2006), has explored the use of digital media to promote creative writing among students from multilingual backgrounds. As one example, primary school students rewrote the Goldilocks story in multiple versions that reflected their own cultural backgrounds (see http://schools.tdsb.on.ca/joyce/main/goldilocks/index.htm). Naqvi (2008), working out of the University of Calgary, has also explored the integration of dual language books into the regular school curriculum and has engaged students in creating their own dual language books (see http://www.rahatnaqvi.ca/). Her website contains a useful database of more than 2,300 published dual language books in over 40 languages, which are all available through the Calgary Public Library system as well as from various commercial publishers.

Common to all of this research is the conviction that pedagogy can transform the lives and academic experience of marginalised students by identifying and challenging exclusionary power structures that have become infused and normalised within the education system.

The next section locates this endeavour within the context of our own research and academic writing. To appropriate the terminology of Rowsell and Pahl (2007): how are our own academic and personal identities sedimented into this textual production? What personal/academic narratives are embedded into this volume?

Our own academic narratives

Cummins. A persistent focus of my research is on literacy development in multilingual school contexts, particularly the relationship between students' home languages and their developing proficiency in the language(s) of instruction. I have also tried to highlight the interactions between societal power relations and teacher-student identity negotiation, arguing that only instruction that explicitly challenges coercive power relations in the wider society will be effective in promoting marginalised group students' academic achievement.

My first publications, which derived from my dissertation at the University of Alberta in 1974, were written from a psycho-educational perspective. I was interested in language and cognition and how exposure to two languages in childhood affected the development of cognitive abilities. In an early paper (Cummins, 1976), I hypothesised that the level of bilingual proficiency students attained mediated the effects of bilingualism on their cognitive and academic development. Thus, the apparent contradiction between early studies (1920s to 1950s) reporting lower cognitive and academic performance among bilingual students, and more recent studies (1960s and 1970s) highlighting the potential cognitive benefits of bilingualism could be resolved by positing two thresholds of proficiency that students needed to attain (a) to avoid the potential negative consequences of instruction through a weaker language, and (b) to experience the enhancement of cognitive and linguistic functioning that knowledge of two or more languages confers on the developing child. In other words, the threshold hypothesis argued that educational treatment interacts with students' academic language proficiency to produce positive or negative educational and cognitive outcomes.

This theoretical work was expanded into the emerging debate on the merits or otherwise of bilingual education. Bilingual programs for minority group students, implemented on a limited scale in contexts such as the US in the 1960s and 1970s, had become highly controversial. Opponents argued that dilution of the instructional time between minority students' first language (L1) and the dominant language (L2) would inevitably result in deficient L2 academic development. I proposed that literacy-related concepts and skills in L1 and L2 are interdependent, or manifestations of a common underlying proficiency, such that academic knowledge and skills transfer across languages under appropriate conditions of development (eg educational support for both languages) (Cummins, 1979). This transfer of concepts and literacy-related skills explains the fact that instruction through a minority language exerts no adverse consequences on students' academic development in the majority language despite less instructional exposure to the majority language. This holds true for students from both minority and majority language backgrounds in various kinds of bilingual programs.

The threshold and interdependence hypotheses together highlight the benefits of encouraging emergent bilingual students to maintain and expand their L1 skills as they acquire L2. In a highly multilingual social context, it is obviously difficult to provide bilingual education opportunities for all groups but, as we try to demonstrate in this book, it *is* possible for teachers to implement bilingual instructional strategies such as the creation of dual language identity texts that will encourage students to use their L1 as a cognitive tool and feel proud of their multilingual talents.

During the same period as the threshold and interdependence hypotheses were being elaborated (late 1970s), I also proposed a distinction between two dimensions of language proficiency – *basic interpersonal communicative skills* (BICS) *and cognitive academic language proficiency* (CALP). This distinction derived from an analysis of more than 400 teacher referral forms and psychological assessments carried out on students who were learning English as an additional language in a western Canadian city. It was clear from the data that students quickly gained conversational fluency in English but took considerably longer to catch up to grade expectations in academic aspects of language (eg vocabulary knowledge, reading comprehension). These data were consistent with previous research in Sweden that had identified the gap between the 'surface fluency' developed by Finnish minority group students in Swedish – their L2 – and the kind of Swedish proficiency required for academic success (see Skutnabb-Kangas, 1984, for a review). A subsequent re-analysis of data from the Toronto Board of Education (Cummins, 1981) showed that, on average, students required 5-7 years to come within a half standard deviation of grade norms on measures of academic language.

In the mid-1980s, my perspective on the achievement of minority group students expanded beyond psycho-educational considerations to incorporate the sociopolitical context. Bilingual education was being rejected in the United States (and elsewhere) because of ideological considerations – such as the claim made by President Reagan in 1981 that it was 'un-American'. Research findings were routinely twisted and spun to conform to these ideological convictions (see Cummins, 2000, 2001 for reviews of this period). It was clear to me that psycho-educational perspectives were incapable of addressing these ideological assumptions about bilingual education, and I began to integrate my interest in bilingualism and bilingual education with a consideration of how power relations affected what was happening in schools.

In 1986, my paper *Empowering Minority Students* was published in the *Harvard Educational Review* and expanded upon in subsequent publications (eg the book *Negotiating Identities: Education for Empowerment in a Diverse Society*, 1996, 2001). This work integrated the previous psycholinguistic analyses and theoretical constructs into a broader framework that linked identity negotiation between teachers and students in the classroom to patterns of power relations in the broader society. I suggested a distinction between coercive and collaborative relations of power which correspond to the common distinction between 'power over' and 'power with'. The former was defined as the exercise of power by a dominant individual, group or country to the detriment of a subordinated individual, group or country. This process is subtractive – the more power one individual or group gets, the less is left for others. By contrast, collaborative relations of power are additive – the more power that accrues to one partner in the relationship, the more there is available for others to share. Based on this distinction, I defined *empowerment* as *the collaborative creation of power*. The implication of this analysis is that any educational reform that seeks to close the achievement gap between students from dominant and marginalised groups will only be effective to the extent that it challenges the operation of coercive relations of power within the school and classroom.

During the past decade, I have had the opportunity to work with educators who have taken initiatives and made instructional choices that have dramatically transformed the identity negotiations going on in classrooms. These educators have constructed diversity as a resource, through a variety of initiatives including enabling multilingual students to create and web-publish dual language books (Chow and Cummins, 2003; Cummins *et al*, 2005; Schecter and Cummins, 2003). These initiatives have demonstrated how bilingual instructional strategies in general, and the creation of identity texts in particular, challenge the implicit devaluation of students' languages and cultures within the school. The case studies described here have been largely inspired by these efforts. What they have in common is a focus on (a) constructing students' bilingualism as a cognitive and personal resource, and (b) affirming students' identities in the process of cultural production.

Early. Growing up in a Scots/Irish, working-class neighbourhood in Scotland, I encountered first-hand coercive relations of power. Throughout my school years, I witnessed how students I knew for sure were able and talented would fail to achieve academically. I never fully understood why, but given that our language use was relentlessly criticised and corrected, I soon intuited it had something to do with the way we spoke and wrote, and what we were inexplicably required to do at school. Mirrors were routinely held up that showed speakers of our particular 'non-standard' variety of English to be less than fully literate or intelligent, and our life options to be limited. Some were devastated by these refracted negative images of self, others resisted. So I came to grasp, very early on, the relationship between language and power in school and the wider society, and the power teachers held over students' self-image. This fuelled my abiding interest in language, learning and constructions of self in the ideological state apparatus of schools (Althusser, 1981).

As a novice teacher in multilingual primary schools in East and North London, I was fortunate that more expert colleagues apprenticed me to empowering language pedagogies. I was especially grateful for being introduced to the practical applications of Michael Halliday's work in functional linguistics. The primary curriculum project, *Breakthrough to Literacy*, and the secondary project, *Language in Use*, were hugely influential in my thinking about how to increase students' awareness of language use in school and society. While frequently unsure of how to proceed, I nevertheless became convinced that not only was it possible to develop a language to talk about language in the classroom but that it was vital to do so critically. As Halliday (1996) states, 'To be literate is not only to participate in the discourse of an information society: it is also to resist it' (p357).

Later, as the ESL consultant on a Vancouver School Board (VSB) district-wide Language across the Curriculum (LAC) Project (1976-79) in the late 1970s, I had an opportunity to collaboratively explore language in subject area learning. By now, I had a graduate degree in language in education, supervised by Bernard Mohan, who works within a Hallidayan tradition of linguistics. Influenced by the Bullock Report (1975) in England, the project was highly innovative. We advocated subject-area-based instruction for ESL learners, which was already in practice in some Vancouver classrooms. We recommended that specialist language teachers work in close liaison with subject-area teachers and that each school establish a policy and plan to address the LAC needs of all learners. The project team produced a series of monographs (Ahrens *et al*, 1978) on goal (activity)-based instruction and the curriculum-cycle, reading, listening, writing, speech and drama, and the arts and language. These monographs remain relevant today. For example, in *The Arts and Language* teachers are advised that, 'a language program that is successful will pay more than lip service to the importance of art, drama and music in the development of language and thought' (1978:14). Moreover, we suggested that '...drawing, diagramming, graphing, constructing models... should be used in combination [with literacy] to develop concepts and higher level thinking' (1978:9). We argued that for all learners, 'language develops best in rich linguistic environments' (1978:16) and that providing intellectually impoverished, linguistically fragmented learning environments for 'at risk' students only served to exacerbate the problem. So, it is disappointing and deplorable that three decades later, arguments for rich, respectful, intellectually challenging language and learning environments, particularly for students marginalised by race, class or ethno-linguistic background, are more urgently required than ever.

From this LAC Project, we learned the challenges entailed by this approach, including the resistance of many subject area teachers to take on the role of explicitly addressing language and literacy in their classroom. We also learned, however, of teachers' desires to promote thinking skills relevant to their subject area and their willingness to use non-verbal modes of representation, particularly still and moving visual images, to engage their students in deep understanding of disciplinary knowledge. So when, on completion of my PhD dissertation on discourse in Social Studies classrooms, I was appointed as the coordinator of ESL for the Province of British Columbia (BC), I bore these lessons in mind when co-authoring a province-wide ESL Resource Book entitled *Integrating Language and Content Instruction* (Early, Thew and Wakefield, 1986).

First, we conducted a Needs Analysis of the thinking-skills required across the curriculum documents from Kindergarten (K) to Grade 12. We then consulted Bernard Mohan to consider how these thinking skills might align with the 'Knowledge Framework' he was then developing, drawing on the perspectives of systemic functional linguistics. Mohan's (1986, 2001) Knowledge Framework is a view of language as discourse in the context of a social practice. In this broad view of learning, 'education is the initiation of the learner into social practices or activities' (Mohan, 2001:110). Mohan proposed that a typical activity, such as conducting an experiment or telling a story, includes (but is not necessarily limited to) six major ways in which knowledge is typically structured in schools. These are classified into two groups: First, the knowledge structures of Description, Sequence and Choice which deal with specific aspects of a situation (ie what a film on the topic might show). The second group deals with general theoretical aspects of the topic (ie those concepts that are not limited to any one time or place). These include: Classifications, Principles (Theoretical Explanations) and Evaluations.

When we iteratively examined the discipline-specific thinking skills we had compiled against Mohan's heuristic, we found that, with few exceptions, they fell into place. Additionally, Mohan argues that knowledge structures can be realised linguistically in texts and tasks and represented visually in 'Key Visuals'. Accordingly, in the resource book we developed (Early, Thew and Wakefield, 1986), we employed these principles of explicit and systematic attention to the integration of language and content learning from a functional (language in context) perspective, including use of visuals as a semiotic tool to mediate/scaffold learning. In collaboration with classroom teachers, we designed (and taught) exemplary projects and units of work that we included in the text.

Shortly after the *BC Ministry Resource Book* (Early, Thew and Wakefield, 1986) and Mohan's seminal *Language and Content* (1986) were published, Mohan and I, who were both at the University of British Columbia, in partnership with the VSB, secured the first of a series of large grants from the BC Ministry of Education (1986-1990) and the Social Sciences Research Council of Canada to research integrated language and content (ILC) teaching in practice, including the affordances of technologies. In this context, Early and Hooper (1987) developed an integrated language and content 'Teaching and Learning Task Model' designed to achieve a number of goals:

- Build students' background knowledge
- Think through topics using visuals and interactive tasks as scaffolds and
- reconstruct knowledge by organising it coherently and cohesively (working across visual and verbal modes) as attention is drawn to technical language use, grammatical structures and the patterns of discourse organisation relative to the topic and the context of situation (see also Mohan, 2001).

A review of research on ILC from the Knowledge Framework perspective is summarised in Early (1992a), Mohan (2001), and Early and Hooper (2001). What has been less explicitly reported from our work at that time is what we encountered regarding the opportunities and challenges of teaching for transfer across L1 and L2 (although see Early, 1992b; Liang, 1999; and Tang, reported in Mohan, 2001). Additionally, interviews with more and less successful ESL students (Early, 1992b) identified the importance of how teachers might foster students' self-confidence, self-esteem, and belief in their own capabilities as one of the key features in fostering students' academic achievement.

The Multiliteracies Project, then, out of which our notion of 'identity texts' emerged, presented itself as an opportunity to expand on our previous work from both LAC and ILC, in the contemporary discourses of globalisation, technological change and knowledge societies. The project afforded us an opportunity to recontextualise, hone and harness the case for pedagogical principles that we, together with our inspirational teacher collaborators and like-minded colleagues, have long been making. These principles assume new urgency and legitimacy in light of 21st century realities such as the new literacies ushered in by evolving technologies, the co-evolving ascendancy of visual and other modes of representation, the economic and social need for multilingual and multiliterate citizens, and increasing recognition that the construction of identities in school and society is crucially important for both individual well-being and the promotion of global citizenship.

Outline of the book

In Chapter 2, we outline the pedagogical principles that have guided our collaborative work with educators. These principles are all grounded in empirical research and are integrated with each other in the form of theoretical frameworks. Rather than presenting just one framework for understanding the pedagogical rationale and impact of identity texts, we have chosen to view the phenomena from different perspectives so we can provide a more layered interpretation and greater opportunities for transforming the research and theory into concrete school-based language policy initiatives. We try to increase the transparency and classroom relevance of the theoretical constructs by illustrating them with concrete examples from an ongoing project in the Toronto area entitled *Engaging Literacies,* in which elementary school-age newcomer students have been using technology to create and present various types of dual language identity texts. Woven into the theoretical frameworks presented in this chapter is a causal model of how schools continue to produce academic failure among marginalised group students and what kinds of educational interventions or changes are likely to reverse this pattern of school failure. We suggest that identity text creation illustrates the kind of pedagogical initiative that is required to get students engaged with literacy and enable them to develop identities of competence.

Chapter 3 focuses on the voices of one teacher and four of her students in the Greater Toronto area who created dual language identity texts in the context of the Multiliteracies Project. Their reflections and insights complement and enrich the theoretical perspectives presented in Chapter 2. We get a clear sense of the multidimensionality of the process of creating dual language identity texts. For example, students talk about how they were able to link their background knowledge to their writing; they explain how they became aware of the differences in the structure of Urdu and English as they discussed how to translate from one language to another; they insightfully discuss how they used their L1 knowledge to help them understand and produce oral and written English; they share their feelings of pride and accomplishment as they recount the reactions of family and friends to their stories. In short, they give voice to the personal transformation they experienced from a school-based identity located in incompetence, defined by their limitations in English ('the ESL student'), to an identity of competence defined by their imagination, creativity and multilingual talents, all of which are mirrored in the identity texts they wrote and published.

Part Two consists of eighteen short vignettes which describe other identity text projects that have been carried out in recent years. These come from a variety of geographic and educational contexts and involve various language configurations and modalities of expression, including American Sign Language (ASL). All these vignettes are accessible in more elaborated form, either on the Internet or in longer publications. We are conscious that the richness of students' and teachers' work cannot be adequately described or presented within the limitations of a linear print-based text such as this one. Our hope is that the short descriptions will encourage readers to explore the fuller accounts, often incorporating complete electronic books and videos, which are available through the Internet.

The final chapter draws together the themes we have explored and points to the future. The pedagogical principles and directions implied by identity text work stand in stark contrast to dominant notions of 'best practice' that are operating in many countries. Issues related to societal power relations and teacher-student identity negotiation are absent from top-down mandates and curriculum dominated by one-size-fits-all standards and external assessment. We highlight the fact that teachers always have pedagogical choices despite the constraints of particular situations. Thus, identity text work is fuelled by teacher agency and is far more evidence-based than conventional approaches that ignore the research linking identity investment to academic achievement among students from marginalised groups. In the final chapter, we also draw on the work of Michael Halliday (1985;1989) to map out linguistic and disciplinary spheres where identity text work can productively be expanded.

What kind of impact can a book like this have?

Most of the case studies documented in this book have involved collaboration between school-based educators and university-based educators. They are examples of what is often called collaborative action research. This kind of research is often dismissed by policy-makers and some researchers as being largely irrelevant to policy and practice. It does not involve large samples of students and teachers, let alone representative samples. Consequently, its generalisability is seen as extremely limited. It also does not involve experimental manipulations of variables whose impact is assessed by comparing treatment and control groups, as is the case with much of the research conducted to assess the impact of medical interventions.

Contrary to these perspectives – often labelled as 'positivist' – we argue that qualitative studies in general, and collaborative action research in particular, are in the mainstream of scientific inquiry (Cummins, 1999, 2007). Scientific inquiry generates knowledge by establishing a set of observed phenomena, forming hypotheses to account for these phenomena, testing these hypotheses against additional data, and gradually refining the hypotheses into more comprehensive theories that have broader explanatory and predictive power. For example, our knowledge of the planetary system and climate patterns derives from this process. Thus qualitative studies in education, together with many forms of quantitative inquiry, establish phenomena that require explanation. They also generate data that can test and refute hypotheses, thereby contributing to the development and refinement of theoretical models.

Our case studies document instances of practice – the events and instructional initiatives described here actually happened. Thus, they represent phenomena that theories and specific hypotheses must be able to explain. For example, if we examine the common assumption (hypothesis) among many second language policy-makers (increasingly less so among researchers) that use of students' L1 should be eliminated or minimised in the teaching of L2, we can ask to what extent this hypothesis is consistent with the phenomena documented in Chapter 3 (and in several of the vignettes in Chapter 4) where the creation of dual language identity texts enabled newcomer students to engage in literacy activities and produce literacy outcomes in the target language (English) that went far beyond what might be expected from typical newcomer students. The credible documentation of these phenomena refutes the hypothesis that L2 outcomes will improve when L1 use is prohibited or minimised. If any hypothesis or theoretical framework is unable to account for the observed phenomena, then it must be rejected or modified to account for the data.

Thus, the instances of practice documented in this volume speak directly to theory – they contribute to the knowledge base relating to literacy and the education of bilingual/EAL students every bit as credibly as any quantitative research. They are in the mainstream of scientific inquiry.

The implications for policy are equally direct. The logic underlying the case studies documented here can be simply stated: actuality implies possibility. If a particular intervention *has* happened, and if particular effects have been observed, then this intervention and its impact *can* happen. The range of case studies in the present volume and the testimony of students, teachers and parents suggest that the narratives summarised in the case studies of Chapter 4 have immense power to effect change both in the instructional choices made by teachers, administrators and policy-makers, and in the identity options opened up to diverse students.

2

Frames of Reference:
Identity Texts in Perspective

Jim Cummins, Margaret Early, Saskia Stille

Anyone who has boarded a plane in the past few years will probably have seen the series of attractive photographs with contrasting labels that adorn the walls of passenger walkways in airports around the world. For example, one of two identical images of an older person may be labelled as 'old' and the second 'wise', inviting the public to question their own assumptions and take account of other perspectives. We experience these reminders about the multiple perspectives and different values that make the world a more complex and culturally richer place courtesy of the Hong Kong and Shanghai Banking Corporation (HSBC) who are attempting to position themselves as both culturally aware and – in their words 'the world's local bank'.

This clever branding strategy has resonance for many of us today because of the obvious need for us to work together across national, cultural, and religious boundaries to solve global economic, environmental and social problems. The insistence that one's own perception is absolutely valid (or that 'truth' has been handed down exclusively to your group) and that other perspectives are therefore invalid is a recipe for futile conflict, whether it applies to ideological beliefs or orientations to scientific research. Currently enlightened scientific inquiry values alternative perspectives – different ways of viewing phenomena – because it is clear that we will get a fuller picture of the total phenomenon when it is viewed from multiple angles and analysed in different ways.

In this chapter, we attempt to frame the phenomenon of identity texts in multiple ways in order to understand its educational relevance more fully. Each framework represents a point of view – what we see from a particular position. When we shift positions, other aspects of the phenomenon that we didn't see clearly before are highlighted or become salient. These different frameworks are not in opposition to each other; they simply reflect different perspectives on the same phenomenon. The function and role of theoretical frameworks in scientific inquiry is elaborated in the next section and the phenomenon of identity texts is then analysed in the context of four different but complementary frameworks, each of which, we believe, contributes some unique aspects to interpreting the phenomenon.

Theoretical frameworks: their contribution to scientific understanding

As noted in Chapter 1, qualitative research is often devalued because the 'gold standard' of research is seen as experimental or quasi-experimental studies in which a 'treatment' or intervention is manipulated in certain ways and its impact assessed in comparison to a control group that has not experienced this treatment. This perspective has been explicitly incorporated into several high-profile research reviews carried out in the US over the past 15 years (eg August and Shanahan, 2006, 2008; National Reading Panel, 2000).

In contrast to this perspective, we argue that ethnographic and case study research is in the mainstream of scientific inquiry, capable not just of generating hypotheses but also of testing and refuting hypotheses. Thus, the theoretical frameworks presented in this chapter derive their scientific credibility from both quantitative and qualitative data that derive from multiple disciplinary perspectives (eg psychology, anthropology, sociology).

There are typically many different ways of organising or interpreting observed phenomena, each of which may be consistent with the empirical data. For example, different disciplines (eg neurology versus cognitive science) may describe and explain the same phenomenon quite differently but in equally valid ways. Also, within a particular discipline, the phenomena may be synthesised legitimately into very different theoretical frameworks depending on the purpose of the framework, the audience envisaged, and the outcomes desired. This process is analogous to observing any object (eg a house): when we move and shift our perspective we see a different image, although the object of our observation has not changed. Thus, theoretical frameworks provide alternative perspectives on particular phenomena in specific contexts and for particular purposes.

Ideally, theoretical frameworks are in constant dialogue with practice. The relationship between theory and practice is two-way and ongoing: practice generates theory, which, in turn, acts as a catalyst for new directions in practice, which then inform theory, and so on. Theory and practice are infused within each other. Theoretical claims or frameworks that integrate these claims are not valid or invalid, true or false; rather, they should be judged by criteria of adequacy and usefulness. 'Adequacy' refers to the extent to which the claims or categories embedded in the framework are consistent with the empirical data and provide a coherent and comprehensive account of the data. 'Usefulness' refers to the extent to which the framework can be used effectively by its intended audience to implement the educational policies and practices it implies or prescribes.

Adequacy and usefulness are never absolutes. More detailed frameworks than those outlined in this chapter may be more 'adequate' in capturing specific details of certain literacy instructional practices. However, gains in specificity or complexity may be made at the expense of usefulness. Too much detail may lead educators and policy-makers to lose sight of the big picture, while excessive theoretical complexity or language that is alien to educators and policy-makers will reduce the likelihood of implementation. So the theoretical frameworks within which the phenomenon of identity texts are considered all extend in two ways: they link with the empirical and theoretical literature on literacy development on the one hand, but they are also grounded in concrete classroom practice, and their purpose is to stimulate sustained dialogue with that practice.

The influence of societal power relations on student achievement

Extensive research has been carried out by sociologists and anthropologists on issues related to ethnicity and educational achievement (eg Bankston and Zhou, 1995; Bishop and Berryman, 2006; McCarty, 2005; 1992; Portes and Rumbaut, 2001; Skutnabb-Kangas, 2000). These studies point clearly to the centrality of societal power relations in explaining patterns of minority group achievement. Groups that experience long-term educational underachievement tend to have experienced material and symbolic violence at the hands of the dominant societal group over generations. Ladson-Billings expresses the point succinctly with respect to African-American students: 'The problem that African-American students face is the constant devaluation of their culture both in school and in the larger society' (1995:485). A direct implication is that in order to reverse this pattern of underachievement, educators, both individually and collectively, must challenge the operation of coercive power relations in the classroom interactions they orchestrate with minority or sub-ordinated group students.

Societal power relations express themselves in the classroom through the process of identity negotiation (Cummins, 2001). The ways in which teachers negotiate identities with students can exert a significant impact on the extent to which students will engage academically or withdraw from academic effort. The intersection of societal power relations and identity negotiation in determining patterns of academic achievement among minority group students is expressed in Figure 2.1.

SOCIETAL POWER RELATIONS
influence
the ways in which educators define their role (teacher identity)
and
the structure of schooling (curriculum, funding, assessment, etc.)

which in turn influence
the ways in which educators interact
with linguistically – culturally-diverse students.

These interactions form
an
INTERPERSONAL SPACE
within which
learning happens
and
identities are negotiated.

These IDENTITY NEGOTIATIONS
either
Reinforce coercive relations of power
or
Promote collaborative relations of power

Figure 2.1: Societal power relations, identity negotiation, and academic achievement

Note. Adapted from *Negotiating identities: Education for empowerment in a diverse society* by J. Cummins 2001, p20.

The framework proposes that relations of power in the wider society, ranging from coercive to collaborative in varying degrees, influence both the ways in which educators define their roles and the types of structures that are established in the educational system. Coercive relations of power refer to the exercise of power by a dominant individual, group or country, to the detriment of a subordinated individual, group or country. For example, over generations and in countries around the world, dominant group institutions (eg schools) have required that subordinated groups deny their social and cultural identities and give up their languages and dialects as a necessary condition for success in the 'mainstream' society.

Collaborative relations of power, by contrast, reflect the sense of the term 'power' that refers to 'being enabled,' or 'empowered' to achieve more. Within collaborative relations of power, 'power' is not a fixed quantity but is generated through interaction with others. The more empowered one individual or group becomes, the more power is generated for others to share. The process is additive rather than subtractive. Within this context, empowerment can be defined as the collaborative creation of power. Students whose schooling experiences reflect collaborative relations of power participate confidently in instruction as a result of their sense of identity being affirmed and extended in their interactions with educators. They also know that their voices will be heard and respected within the classroom. Schooling amplifies rather than silences their power of self-expression.

Educator role definitions refer to the mindset of expectations, assumptions and goals that educators bring to the task of educating socially and culturally diverse students. Educational structures refer to the organisation of schooling in a broad sense that includes policies, programmes, curriculum and assessment. While these structures will generally reflect the ideologies, values and priorities of dominant groups in society, they are by no means fixed or static. As with most other aspects of the way societies are organised and resources distributed, educational structures are contested and resisted by individuals and groups.

Educational structures, together with educator role definitions, determine the patterns of interactions between educators, students, and communities. These interactions form an interpersonal space within which the acquisition of knowledge and formation of identity are negotiated. Power is created and shared within this interpersonal space where minds and identities meet. As such, these teacher-student interactions constitute the most immediate determinant of student academic success or failure. Newman, Griffin, and Cole (1989) label this interpersonal space 'the construction zone'. The framework (Figure 2.1) argues that teacher-student collaboration in the construction of knowledge will operate effectively only in contexts where students' identities are being affirmed. Essentially, this conception extends Vygotsky's (1978) notion of the zone of proximal development beyond the cognitive sphere into the realms of affective development and power relationships. It makes clear that the construction zone can also be a constriction zone where student identities and learning are constricted rather than extended.

The interactions between educators, students and communities are never neutral; to varying degrees they either reinforce coercive relations of power or promote collaborative relations of power. In the former case, they contribute to the disempowerment of culturally diverse students and communities; in the latter case, the interactions constitute a process of empowerment that enables educators, students and communities to challenge the operation of coercive power structures.

The operation of the processes depicted in this framework can be seen in the research of Bishop and Berryman (2006) which explored patterns of educational engagement among Maori youth in Aoteroa/New Zealand. Very different perspectives on causes of student engagement (or lack thereof) emerged from interviews with educators, the students themselves, and community members. Bishop and Berryman describe the varying perspectives as follows:

> A large proportion of the teachers we interviewed took a position from which they explained Maori students' lack of educational achievement in deficit terms [ie Maori students themselves and their homes]. This gave rise to low expectations of Maori students' ability or a fatalistic attitude in the face of 'the system', creating a downward-spiralling, self-fulfilling prophecy of low Maori student achievement and failure. In terms of agency, this is a helpless position to take, because it means that there is very little any individual teacher can do about the achievement of the Maori students in his or her classroom. (p261)
>
> ....
>
> In contrast, the students, their *whanau* [family], and their principals most commonly identified the major influences on Maori students' educational achievement as coming under the broad heading of 'relationships and interactions'. Those who take this position are putting forward explanations based on the power differentials and imbalances between the various participants in the relationships and focusing on how they can and must be managed better. (p263)

Bishop and Berryman (2006) point out that 'most Maori people, young and older, spoke passionately about their desires to achieve within the educational system and that they were just as adamant that this should not be at the expense of their Maori identity' (p264). They highlight the influence of the 'imagery' that teachers hold of Maori children:

> Simply put, if the imagery held of Maori children (or indeed of any children) and the resulting interaction patterns stem from deficits and pathologies, then teachers' principles and practices will reflect this, and the educational crisis for Maori students will be perpetuated. (p263)

They point out that effective instruction challenges the devaluation of Maori identity in the school and wider society. The elements of effective instruction 'involve the teacher creating a culturally appropriate and responsive learning context, where young people can engage in learning by bringing their prior cultural knowledge and experiences to classroom interactions, which legitimate these, instead of ignoring or rejecting them' (p264-265).

Within the context of this empowerment framework, the function of identity text creation as a challenge to coercive relations of power is clear. When a dominant language is used as a medium of instruction, bilingual students from socially marginalised communities are frequently given the message – implicitly or explicitly – that they should leave their L1 at the schoolhouse door. Although the message may be rationalised in different ways, the coercive intent is equally evident whether it is targeted at Tibetan-speaking students in Tibet, Xhosa-speaking students in South Africa, Turkish-speaking students in Germany or the UK, or Urdu-speaking students in Toronto. By contrast, dual language identity texts clearly proclaim the legitimacy of students' multilingual skills and showcase their intellectual, literary and artistic talents. They generate power for both students and teachers.

How does a pedagogy focused on the collaborative creation of power relate to broader orientations to pedagogy that characterise contemporary educational discourse in different countries? We consider this issue next.

Identity texts in the context of broader pedagogical orientations

Various orientations to pedagogy can be distinguished in the extensive literature on teaching that has accrued over the past century (eg Barnes, 1976; Dewey, 1916; Freire, 1970). Different terms have been used by different theorists and the pedagogical options have frequently been discussed as oppositional binaries (eg teacher-centred versus child-centred instruction; traditional versus progressivist pedagogy, phonics versus whole-language; 'banking' education versus liberatory education, etc). We have attempted to capture the range of pedagogical options that have been proposed in the literature by distinguishing among transmission, social constructivist and transformative orientations (Cummins, 2004; Skourtou, Kourtis Kazoullis and Cummins, 2006). We view these three pedagogical orientations as nested within each other rather than as distinct and isolated from each other.

Transmission-oriented pedagogy is represented in the inner circle with the narrowest focus. The goal is to transmit information and skills specified in curriculum (and in tests) directly to students. The importance of activating students' prior knowledge and developing learning strategies may be acknowledged within transmission or direct instruction approaches. However, in practice, activation of students' prior knowledge is often operationally defined as re-visiting content and skills that were taught in previous lessons. Similarly, learning strategy instruction tends to be narrowly focused on the content of particular lessons rather than integrated into a broader process of collaborative inquiry and knowledge generation.

Social constructivist pedagogy, occupying the middle pedagogical space, acknowledges the relevance of transmission of information and skills but broadens this focus to include the development among students of higher-order thinking abilities based on teachers and students co-constructing knowledge and understanding. The focus is on experiential learning, collaborative inquiry and knowledge building. Theorists who endorse social constructivist or sociocultural approaches to pedagogy tend to build on Vygotsky's (1978) foundational work. The influential synthesis of the research on learning carried out by Bransford, Brown and Cocking (2000) is very much social constructivist in its emphasis on integrating factual knowledge with conceptual frameworks, activating students' pre-existing knowledge, and enabling students to take active control of the learning process through the development of metacognitive strategies.

Finally, transformative approaches to pedagogy broaden the focus still further by emphasising the relevance not only of transmitting the curriculum and constructing knowledge but also of enabling students to gain insight into how knowledge intersects with power. Transformative pedagogy uses collaborative critical inquiry to enable students to analyse and understand the social realities of their own lives and of their communities. Students discuss, and frequently act on, ways in which these realities might be transformed through various forms of social action. The goal is to promote critical literacy among students, with a focus on social realities relevant to issues of equity and social justice. In other words, transformative pedagogy enables students to scrutinise and actively challenge patterns of power relations in the broader society. Transformative approaches typically draw their inspiration from the

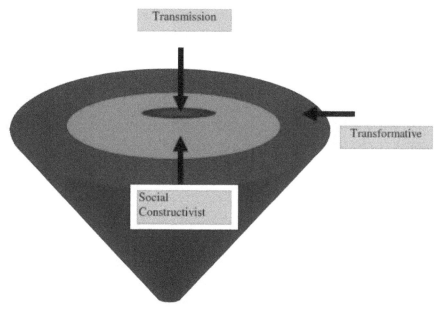

Figure 2.2: Nested pedagogical orientations (Vasilia Kourtis-Kazoullis)

work of Freire (1970) while also acknowledging the important influence of Vygotsky (1978).

The rationale for nesting these orientations within each other is to highlight the fact that features of transmission pedagogy are relevant to all kinds of learning. In classrooms that are clearly transmission-orientated, as well as in communities of critical inquiry among students and teachers, explicit instruction and structured guidelines can play an important role in effective teaching and learning. Transmission of information and skills becomes problematic only when it constitutes the predominant or even exclusive focus of instruction. Exclusive reliance on transmission pedagogy is likely to entail promotion of memorisation rather than learning for deep understanding, passive rather than active learning and minimal activation of students' prior knowledge. Similarly, a transformative orientation is not in any way opposed either to transmission of curriculum content or the co-construction of knowledge between teachers and students. Rather it builds on and expands transmission and social constructivist approaches in order to pursue a wider variety of pedagogical goals and a broader educational vision.

The nested pedagogical orientations framework outlined above is compatible with the multiliteracies instructional framework proposed by the The New London Group (1996). Their framework highlighted the importance of situated practice, overt instruction, critical framing, and transformed practice.

The essence of this framework is that students should be given opportunities to engage in meaningful experience and practice within a learning community, and the development of concepts and understanding should be supported by explicit instruction as required. Students should have opportunities to step back from what they have learned and examine concepts and ideas critically in relation to their social relevance. Finally, they should be given opportunities to take the knowledge they have gained further – to put it into play in the world of ideas and come to understand how their insights can exert an impact on people and issues in the real world. Situated practice and overt instruction correspond to social constructivist and transmission orientations respectively, while critical framing and transformed practice represent elements of a transformative orientation.

Most national efforts at educational reform over the past 20 years (eg in the UK and US) have tended to focus on increasing the efficiency of transmission of content and skills, particularly for students from low-income backgrounds who are seen to be 'at risk'. From our perspective, the reason these attempts at educational reform that were aimed at closing the achievement gap have had so little impact is that they have typically stayed within the realm of transmission approaches to pedagogy. Predominant reliance on transmission approaches contravenes core principles of learning (as documented by Bransford, Brown and Cocking, 2000) and also fails to address some of the fundamental causes of marginalised students' underachievement which, as noted earlier, are rooted in the operation of societal power relations in schools and in the wider society.

Social constructivist approaches indirectly address some aspects of societal power relations and identity negotiation. In comparison to transmission approaches, social constructivism generates an expanded image of the student. Students are seen as capable of higher-order thinking and their cultural experience and prior knowledge are likely to be actively mobilised. However, the rationale for this orientation tends to be justified with respect to cognitive dimensions of learning rather than in terms of how societal power relations affect learning. Thus, social constructivist approaches may create contexts of empowerment for marginalised group students (understood in terms of developing identities of competence (Manyak, 2004)), but the empowerment is limited by virtue of its individual rather than social focus. Only transformative orientations explicitly address the role of societal power relations in generating underachievement. The focus on creating contexts of empowerment directly challenges the operation of coercive relations of power in schools and society.

In short, as used in the present framework, the defining criterion of transformative pedagogy is that teacher-student classroom interactions challenge the operation of coercive relations of power. Interactions that meet this criterion include

- an explicit instructional focus on social justice and equity by means of critical analysis of social issues and texts (broadly defined) and
- classroom project work (such as identity text creation), associated with the students' cultural and linguistic capital, which promotes identities of competence among students from marginalised community groups, thereby challenging the devaluation of these students' cultures and languages in the wider society.

Within the framework, the pedagogical orientations are nested within each other and merge into each other along an expanding continuum characterised by increasing instructional inclusion of social justice and equity concerns.

Two other frameworks are outlined in the following sections. Each focuses on instructional considerations in greater detail than is the case with the Empowerment and Pedagogical Orientations frameworks. The Literacy Expertise framework incorporates the notion of the pedagogical space for knowledge generation and identity negotiation created in teacher-student interactions but also specifies some central dimensions of language pedagogy that contribute to the development of academic language expertise. The Literacy Engagement framework shifts focus to the instructional conditions necessary to promote strong literacy attainment among emergent bilingual students. It highlights research supporting the roles of literacy engagement and identity affirmation in promoting literacy attainment, both of which have been largely ignored by policy-makers ostensibly concerned with closing the achievement gap between low-income and higher-income students.

The Literacy Expertise framework

Consistent with the account of how power relations operate (Figure 2.1), the Literacy Expertise framework (Figure 2.3) posits that teacher-student interactions create an interpersonal space within which knowledge is generated and identities are negotiated. Students' literacy development will be optimised when these interactions maximise both cognitive/literacy engagement and identity investment. There is overwhelming evidence, reviewed below, that literacy engagement is a direct determinant of literacy attainment. However, identity investment is equally important. Students will actively engage with literacy only when that engagement is identity-affirming. Thus, if students are seen by teachers, and consequently come to see themselves, as not being particularly bright academically, they will tend to disengage from academic effort because such effort simply reinforces an identity of incompetence in this sphere.

Norton (2000; in press) has insightfully highlighted the role of identity investment in second language learning and similar processes are at work in academic engagement generally. She notes that, unlike the construct of *motivation*, which is a psychological attribute of the individual, *investment* is a sociological construct which views the language learner as having a complex identity that changes across time and space and is directly affected by patterns of social interaction and societal power relations. Viewed from this perspective, identity texts represent an instructional tool that transforms the interpersonal space within the classroom to enable students (particularly those from marginalised social groups) to develop and showcase identities of competence linked to literacy and academic work generally.

The Literacy Expertise framework attempts to express in a concrete way the kinds of instructional emphases and language interactions required to build students' literacy expertise. Optimal instruction will include a Focus on Meaning, a Focus on Language, and a Focus on Use. The focus on meaning entails not just understanding content but also developing critical literacy rather than just processing text at surface level. The focus on language involves (a) promoting explicit knowledge of how the linguistic system operates, (b) developing a metalanguage to talk about it, and (c) enabling students to become critically aware of how language operates within society. If students are to participate effectively within a democratic society they should be able to 'read' how language is used to achieve social goals: to elucidate issues, to persuade, to deceive, to include, to exclude, etc. The focus on use component parallels the New London Group's transformed practice but expresses much more concretely what this might look like within the classroom context. It argues that optimal instruction will enable students to generate knowledge, create literature and art and act on social realities, using a wide range of linguistic registers, including academic ones. All of these forms of academic engagement can find expression in identity texts.

The Literacy Expertise framework also makes explicit the fact that classroom instruction always positions students in ways that reflect the implicit – or sometimes explicit – image of the student in the teacher's mind. How students are positioned either expands or constricts their opportunities for identity

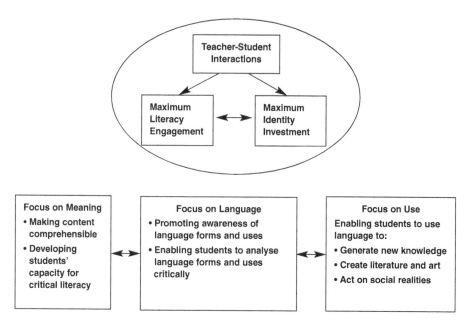

Figure 2.3: The Literacy Expertise framework

Note. Adapted from Negotiating identities: Education for empowerment in a diverse society by J. Cummins 2001, p125.

investment and cognitive engagement. With respect to the nested pedagogical orientations in Figure 2.1, these orientations can be seen as representing a continuum ranging from relatively constricted to more expanded opportunities for identity investment and cognitive engagement.

The Literacy Engagement framework

The Literacy Engagement framework (Figure 2.4) was articulated to highlight the empirical evidence linking the construct of print access (Lindsay, 2010) and literacy engagement (Guthrie, 2004) to the development of reading comprehension. Guthrie notes that the construct of literacy engagement incorporates notions of time on task (reading extensively), affect (enthusiasm and enjoyment of literacy), depth of cognitive processing (strategies to deepen comprehension), and active pursuit of literacy activities (amount and diversity of literacy practices in and out of school). He points out that engaged readers are active and energised in reading and use their minds with an emphasis on either cognitive strategies or conceptual knowledge. Furthermore, he notes that engaged reading is often socially interactive insofar as engaged students are capable of discussion or sharing with friends despite the fact that much of their reading may be solitary.

The research basis for specifying literacy engagement as a strong predictor of literacy achievement comes from numerous studies linking access to print and extensive reading with reading comprehension (for reviews see Krashen, 2004; Lindsay, 2010) as well as the large-scale data from the Organisation for Economic Cooperation and Development's (OECD) Programme for International Student Assessment (PISA). The PISA studies showed that 'the level of a student's reading engagement is a better predictor of literacy performance than his or her socioeconomic background, indicating that cultivating a student's interest in reading can help overcome home disadvantages' (OECD, 2004:8).

Literacy engagement is logically dependent on students' access to print. A recent review of the impact of this construct on students' literacy achievement revealed a strong causal impact.

> The results of this meta-analytic review provide firm support for consistent and reliable relationships between children's access to print material and outcomes. Separate meta-analytic procedures performed on just those effects produced by 'rigorous' studies suggest that children's access to print materials plays a causal role in facilitating behavioural, educational, and psychological outcomes in children- especially attitudes toward reading, reading behaviour, emergent literacy skills, and reading performance. (Lindsay, 2010:85)

The framework also specifies four broad instructional dimensions that are critical to enabling emergent bilingual students to engage actively with literacy from an early stage in their learning of English. Typically, newcomer students who arrive in the host country after the early grades are delayed several years before they can engage actively with L2 reading and writing at their cognitive and chronological age level. This is because age-appropriate L2 reading materials are beyond their comprehension in the early stages of learning and their L2 proficiency is inadequate to write extensively and

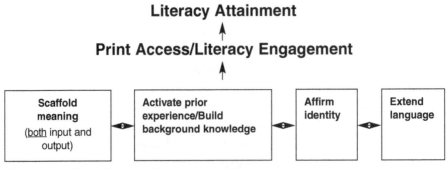

Figure 2.4: The Literacy Engagement framework.

coherently in their L2. Numerous studies (reviewed in Cummins, 2001) from several countries show that, on average, at least five years is required for immigrant students to catch up academically.

The core propositions that underlie the framework can be stated as follows: In order to teach emergent bilingual students effectively, teachers need to maximise their opportunities to become actively engaged with reading and writing. Literacy engagement will be enhanced when

- students' ability to understand and use academic language is supported through specific instructional strategies,
- their prior experience and current knowledge are activated,
- their identities are affirmed, and
- their knowledge of, and control over, language is extended across the curriculum.

The distinctions captured in the framework are frequently fused in classroom practice. For example, acknowledging and activating students' prior experience simultaneously affirms the legitimacy of that experience and, by extension, the legitimacy of students' identities. Student identity is also affirmed when they are encouraged to use their L1 writing abilities as a stepping stone to writing in L2.

Scaffold meaning. Generally associated with the work of Bruner and of Vygostky, the term 'scaffolding', refers to the provision of temporary supports that enable learners to carry out tasks and perform academically at a higher level than they would be capable of without these supports (Gibbons, 2002). Activation of students' prior experience and building background knowledge is one form of scaffolding that operates on students' internal cognitive structures. Others focus on modifying and mediating the input so that it becomes more comprehensible to students. These include the use of visuals, demonstrations, dramatisation, acting out meanings, interactive and collaborative tasks and explicit explanation of words, linguistic structures and discourse patterns. Scaffolding also supports students to use the target language in both written and oral modes. For example, our research in the context of the Multi-literacies Project has demonstrated how bilingual instructional strategies such as encouraging newcomer students to write initially in their L1 and then work with teachers, peers and/or community volunteers to create an English version results in significantly more accomplished English performance than if students had been confined to using only English (Cummins *et al*, 2005).

This process is illustrated by the case of Khadija, who arrived in Toronto from Afghanistan in the middle of the school year. Khadija was already bilingual in Dari and Pashto but spoke no English when she arrived. As part of the *Engaging Literacies* project, her grade five class was writing digital dual-language story books about themselves at the time on topics such as *All about me* and *My journey to Canada*. Because Khadija was only just beginning to acquire English language, we encouraged her to write her story entirely in Dari. Her same-language peers assisted by explaining the activity to her, and her teachers used her L1 story to scaffold her English language development by assisting her to add English labels and text where possible. Khadija wrote a long, detailed narrative about her Afghani home and holidays, which clearly would have been impossible for her to do in English at this early stage of English language acquisition. A sample page from Khadija's story is presented in Figure 2.5.

Activate prior experience/build background knowledge. Effective instruction for all students activates their prior experience and builds background knowledge as needed. Learning can be defined as *the integration of new knowledge or skills with the knowledge or skills we already possess*. Therefore it is crucial to activate students' pre-existing knowledge so that they can relate new information to what they already know. Snow, Burns and Griffin (1998) express the centrality of background knowledge as follows:

> Every opportunity should be taken to extend and enrich children's background knowledge and understanding in every way possible, for the ultimate significance and memorability of any word or text depends on whether children possess the background knowledge and conceptual sophistication to understand its meaning. (p219)

This implies that when emergent bilingual students' background knowledge is encoded in their L1, they should be encouraged to use their L1 to activate and extend this knowledge – for example by brainstorming in groups, writing in L1 as a stepping stone to writing in L2, carrying out Internet research in their L1.

The following example from the *Engaging Literacies* project illustrates how common curricular topics, in this case differences and similarities between urban and rural communities, can be linked to multilingual students' prior experience. Rather than working exclusively from the school textbooks for this topic, the teachers and researchers engaged students in exploring aspects of their local community and the communities where they or their families had lived. We used Google Earth to zoom into and capture images of places where the students were from and noted whether these places had characteristics of urban or rural communities. This activity enabled students to connect what they knew about their communities to new concepts in English.

The activity also illuminated how students' experiences map onto their knowledge construction and meaning-making. For instance, we found that the binary urban-rural distinction displayed in the school textbooks bore little reality to some students' lived experience. Students grappled with questions such as: Does Kabul look like a rural or urban community when there

Figure 2.5: Sample page from Khadija's story

What is a community? A place where people live, work, and share the same interests.		
Compare	**Our Community:**	**Another Community:** Pakistan karachi
Housing	Apartment buildings	Houses with huge balconeys
Transportation	Cars Trucks vehei Public bus	moter cycles vans Cars vehecils bycides
Environment	It's nice beautiful flowers freash air	Some places have a lot of nature and some don't lots of flowers rocky ground
Land use and stluctuls	buildings parking lots roads 3 schools	lots of markets and roads with lots of parking lots.
Recreational facilities	school playgound	beautiful parks
Population	high population	Some places high population Some places low population

Figure 2.6. Graphic organiser comparing communities

are unpaved roads and few high rise buildings in the city? The image above shows one student's graphic organiser comparing features of communities in the cities of Karachi, Pakistan, and Toronto, Canada (Figure 2.6).

Affirm identity. As noted above, identity affirmation is crucial for literacy engagement. Students who feel their culture and identity validated in the classroom are much more likely to engage with literacy than those who feel that their culture and identity are ignored or devalued. Students' perceptions of their intelligence, imagination, and multilingual talents are a part of their

Figure 2.7: Students making a digital film about their community

identity and when these are affirmed in the school and classroom context, they invest their identities actively in the learning process. The affirmation of identity in the context of teacher-student interactions explicitly challenges the devaluation of student and community identity in the wider society.

The increasing accessibility of powerful technologies provides teachers and students with new ways of creating and showcasing students' multimodal identity texts. We used digital video and photography and iMovie software with a grade 3 teacher and his 10 year old students, to produce a short digital film about the school community. Through interviews with the students, parents and teacher, the film makes visible the unique experiences of the multilingual children and newcomer families. The students added voiceovers and narratives to help the audience understand their perspectives on the school community. As an identity text, the film promoted identities of competence among these students. They used sophisticated technology, made insightful observations, and helped create a cultural artefact far beyond what they or their parents dreamed possible. Figure 2.7 shows students involved in making the film, and Figure 2.8 shows screen shots from several sections of the film.

Extend language. As students progress through the grades, they are required to read increasingly complex texts in the content areas of the curriculum – science, mathematics, social studies, literature. The complexity of academic language reflects:

Figure 2.8: Screen shots from iMovie software used in making the digital film

- the difficulty of the concepts that students are required to understand
- the vocabulary load in content texts that include many low frequency and technical words that we almost never use in typical conversation, and
- increasingly sophisticated grammatical constructions (eg passive voice) and patterns of discourse organisation that again are almost never used in everyday conversational contexts.

Students are not only required to read this language, they must also use it in writing reports, essays, and other forms of school work. Thus, in order to develop students' academic language, it is essential to provide explicit instruction in each discipline's textual practices and ways of using language. Once again, bilingual instructional strategies – for example drawing attention to cognate relationships, encouraging students to compare and contrast L1 and L2 – can enhance bilingual students' awareness of language and how it operates.

The following example illustrates how students' L1 competences can be easily integrated into regular curriculum activities with the result that stu-

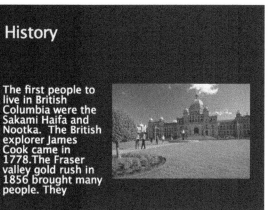
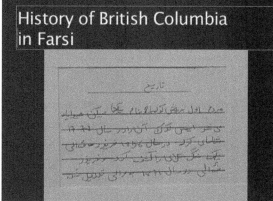

Figure 2.9: Sample slides from student presentation, in English and in Farsi, on the Canadian province of British Columbia

dents' attention is drawn to the connections between L1 and English. Newcomer students were engaged in researching the Canadian provinces as part of their grade 4 social studies curriculum. They gathered information from the Internet and from books in the school library, and prepared PowerPoint presentations to share what they learned with classmates and parents. They were encouraged to use their L1 at every stage of the project, from planning and researching, to writing and delivering their presentations in front of an audience. The students learned not only to search for and locate information but also to authenticate and synthesise the information, and to use text features such as slide titles and images to help display their findings. The sample slides shown here were researched and created by Asad, whose first language is Farsi. Although the English vocabulary and syntax in the text was complex, the student planned and discussed his presentation with other students in Farsi, which assisted him in understanding and adding the information from the Internet sources into his own presentation in English.

Conclusion

The pedagogical significance of identity text creation can be highlighted within each of the four frameworks outlined in this chapter. Within the Empowerment framework, the inclusion of students' L1 as a resource for learning within the classroom challenges coercive power structures that position students' bilingualism as irrelevant to academic achievement or as an obstacle to the learning of the dominant school language. Furthermore, in the process of creating dual language identity texts, students and teachers are negotiating identities in such a way that power is being generated for both. Students formerly seen as 'ESL' and as having little to say or contribute within the classroom are now enabled to showcase their linguistic, intellectual, and creative talents, thereby repudiating the inferior status frequently occupied in the wider society by their communities.

The Pedagogical Orientations framework highlights the fact that a transformative orientation challenges coercive relations of power while at the same time incorporating aspects of transmission and social constructivist approaches. In the context of identity text creation by students, teachers will certainly transmit extensive information about effective writing (eg conventions such as headings and punctuation, coherence and organisation, etc); they will also work with students to co-construct insights and knowledge, as emphasised within a social constructivist approach. However, identity text project work makes linkages between what is happening in the classroom and broader patterns of power relations in school and society. Its transformative potential derives from the fact that it explicitly challenges the devaluation of bilingual and marginalised students' cultures and languages in the wider society.

The Literacy Expertise framework highlights the fact that identity negotiation within the classroom is just as crucial for student engagement and learning as any of the instructional strategies that focus narrowly on cognitive aspects of learning. Identity text production incorporates all three dimensions of language highlighted in the framework. Students are focused on meaning insofar as they are investing their identities in creating 'texts' (cultural productions) that will be shared with a variety of audiences. In the process of creating these texts, students must focus directly on language and become aware of how to use language effectively as a tool for communication. This process is explicitly highlighted by Kanta in the next chapter in relation to the extensive metalinguistic discussion that took place among the three authors of 'The New Country' as they struggled to translate from Urdu to English and English to Urdu. The Focus on Use dimension is reflected in the reality that when teachers expand the pedagogical space from a monolingual to a multilingual zone, even newcomer students with minimal English can use language to generate new knowledge, create literature and art, and act on social realities.

Finally, the Literacy Engagement framework highlights the fact that print access/literacy engagement is a stronger predictor of literacy attainment than is socioeconomic status. What better way to get students from marginalised communities engaged with literacy than to enable them to create their own texts and take ownership of this process? For newcomer students, scaffolding is enabled by encouraging them to use their L1 for initial writing and then finding ways to support them in translating from L1 to L2. These supports may come from teachers, bilingual assistants, bilingual peers, or community volunteers who speak students' L1.

Technology may also be helpful in supporting students to translate their writing from L1 to L2. For example, students could use a computer to write in L1, or enter their work into a word processor after initial writing by hand, and then paste the writing into Google language tools, or some other machine translation system, for translation into English. The translation will probably be approximate but is usually sufficient to give the teacher the gist of what the student is writing about. Then the teacher or a group of classroom peers can work with the newcomer student to edit and refine the English version and publish both L1 and English versions in the form of a dual language book. Obviously, this process is also tapping into students' prior and current knowledge, affirming their identities, and extending their awareness of how language works.

The conceptual tools outlined in this chapter come into further dialogue with actual classroom practice in the next chapter. We present the 'insider' perspectives of Lisa Leoni and four of her students as they reflect on the process and impact of identity text production.

3

'I'm not just a coloring person': Teacher and Student Perspectives on Identity Text Construction

Lisa Leoni, Sarah Cohen, Jim Cummins,
Vicki Bismilla, Madiha Bajwa, Sulmana Hanif,
Kanta Khalid, Tomer Shahar

Introduction

In this chapter, Lisa Leoni and four of her students reflect on the process of constructing dual language identity texts. They document the changes in student self-image and quality of learning that come about when the teacher encourages students to use their home languages as cognitive tools and resources for learning and thereby repudiate the implicit 'English-only zone' policies that characterise most classrooms.

Three of the students (Madiha, Sulmana, and Kanta) were in Lisa's Grade 7/8 (ages 13 and 14) classroom during the 2003/2004 academic year. The following year, Madiha and Tomer were members of Lisa's ESL class. In both contexts, students carried out projects using their L1s together with English. This approach was not at all typical in Canadian schools at the time. Despite a national policy that endorses multiculturalism as a positive force within Canadian society, there has been little sustained policy discussion with respect to the pedagogical implications of linguistic diversity. The topic is largely absent from principals' courses and from pre-service teacher education courses. Prominent books on school leadership and the management of educational change say nothing about the issue. In short, home languages other than English or French have been viewed as largely irrelevant to children's schooling. At best, they are treated with benign neglect and ignored; at worst, educators consider them an obstacle to the acquisition of English or French and discourage their use in school and at home.

The collaboration took place over the course of a year and a half, during which the school-based researcher (Lisa Leoni) and the university-based researcher (Sarah Cohen) were in close contact and the university researcher made weekly visits to the school. The information Sarah gathered included classroom observations during which field notes were taken, audio and video recording of classes, and semi-structured interviews with Lisa and her students. Lisa was responsible for implementing the dual language practices that were the focus of the collaboration, for collecting samples of student work and for distributing questionnaires about language use.

Shortly after her arrival in Canada, Madiha Bajwa, a student in Lisa's Grade 7 class, authored a bilingual Urdu-English book entitled *The New Country* with two of her friends, Kanta Khalid and Sulmana Hanif. The 20-page book, illustrated with the help of classmate Jennifer Du, 'describes how hard it was to leave our country and come to a new country.' Both Kanta and Sulmana had arrived in Toronto in Grade 4 and were reasonably fluent in English but Madiha was in the very early stages of acquiring English.

The three girls collaborated in writing *The New Country* in the context of a unit on the theme of migration that integrated social studies, language, and ESL curriculum expectations. They researched and wrote the story over several weeks, sharing their experiences and language skills. Madiha's English was minimal but her Urdu was fluent. Sulmana was fluent and literate in both Urdu and English. Kanta's home language was Punjabi and she had attended an English-medium school in Pakistan. She had acquired much of her Urdu since arriving in Toronto and had become highly skilled in switching back and forth between Urdu and English. In composing the story, the three girls discussed their ideas primarily in Urdu but wrote the initial draft in English. Sulmana acted as scribe for both languages.

Like Madiha, Tomer Shahar came into Lisa's ESL class with minimal English. The opportunity to write in Hebrew and to work from Hebrew to English enabled him to build on his knowledge and experience, and to share his interests, particularly his passion for horses, with his teacher and peers. Figure 3.1 shows the covers of *The New Country*, written by Kanta, Madiha and Sulmana, and *Tom Goes to Kentucky*, written by Tomer. These and other dual language identity texts can be viewed at http://www.multiliteracies.ca/index.php/folio/viewProject/8.

Figure 3.1. Covers of The New Country and Tom Goes to Kentucky

In a more typical classroom, Tomer's and Madiha's ability to gain access to the curriculum and carry out grade-appropriate work would have been severely limited by their minimal knowledge of English. They certainly would not have been in a position to write extensively in English about their experiences, ideas, and insights. But when the social structure of the classroom was changed in very simple ways, both students were enabled to express them-selves in ways that few newcomer students experience. Their home lan-guages, in which all their experiences, including immigration, were encoded, became once again a tool for learning.

The perspectives of Lisa as the teacher implementing a radically different approach to supporting language and literacy development across the curri-culum and of Kanta, Madiha, Sulmana, and Tomer, the students who ex-perienced this approach, are presented in the following pages. They were recorded at various stages of the project, in interviews and conversation, as well as during the presentation made by the authors of this chapter at the Ontario Teachers of English as a Second Language (TESL) conference in October 2005 (a webcast with excerpts of these presentations can be viewed at www.curriculum.org/secretariat/december7.html). These perspectives are organised according to themes. The quotes retain their 'oral' character with minimal editing.

Lisa's Instructional Philosophy

Identity affirmation and expansion. The way I see it, everything has to relate to the identity of the students; children have to see themselves in every aspect of their work at school.

My overarching goal as a teacher is to uncover all that is unknown to me about my students – linguistically and culturally, and especially to understand the community they are part of – their parents, their friends, their faith – and the list goes on. So when a student enters my class, I want to discover all I can about that student as a learner and as a person.

What I love about using identity texts as a teaching strategy is that it validates students' cultural and linguistic identities. The texts also help connect what students are learning in the class to their lived experiences and when these connections happen, learning becomes real for them because they are using their language and culture for purposes that have relevance for them. Most importantly, they end up owning the work they produce.

The book, *The New Country*, was written by Kanta, Sulmana and Madiha when we were studying a unit on migration. It represents the immigration story of all three girls. As they worked on this project I was able to learn about their skill levels, the roles played by each in the writing and development of the story, socially and academically, and the overall learning process, even when the interactions were happening in their first language. There was a lot of evidence of metalinguistic negotiation, cognitive engagement and cooperative processing of ideas.

Like any new student, Madiha was part of my classroom from day one. Language and cultural differences in the classroom became naturalised, so the non-Urdu speaking students saw this as an accepted and valid part of the learning process and it removed the stigma of the students being 'ESL students'.

I called Kanta and Sulmana my co-educators. This experience also created a learning situation for them because they modeled literacy practices and they themselves also moved along the continuum of ESL skill levels. At the time they were writing the book, they were placed at stage 3 but after only a few months, they started demonstrating stage 4 capabilities. This was facilitated in large part because this collaborative process allowed Kanta and Sulmana to be the educators, to take that leadership role.

The three girls also showed greater interest and confidence in school. They participated more frequently in school-wide events, became more involved in class and more willing to share work with their peers. Overall, they became happier and more engaged in school.

Teaching for transfer – It's been clear to me that students learning an additional language use their first language to help them make sense not only of grammatical structures or concepts represented by vocabulary but also of the world around them, whether they are given the opportunity or not. What is inside a language helps students see what they see, and draw connections between old learning and new. So rather than keeping this a hidden process, my aim is to give it a space in the classroom. Opportunities like writing a dual language book bring out the inner voice of students and make visible to the teacher what is usually invisible.

Inclusion and assessment – When Tomer entered my class last year, much of the work he produced was in Hebrew. Why? Because that is where his knowledge was encoded and I wanted to make sure that Tomer was an active participant in my class. It was also a way for me to gain insight into his level of literacy and oral language development. As I watched him carry out various writing tasks, it became clear to me that Tomer had very strong literacy skills in his first language. For example, when I asked him to do a creative writing piece based on three pictures that he himself could select, his pencil didn't stop moving, there was little hesitation, and it was apparent that his ideas flowed easily. Next I had him read aloud to me [in Hebrew] what he had written and there I saw the fluency, intonation, and the ease with which he read. I was able to relate his oral language and literacy skills to the English language development rubric that I follow for assessing student progress.

The next step I followed was accessing a resource within my school: a teacher who could read Hebrew. And so as she read [the English translation], I typed. You can see the paragraph formation, features of a narrative account that are satisfied, and well-developed vocabulary. Everything's there that I'm looking for in my English-speaking students, so again it was clear to me that Tomer had all the skills that I was looking for: reasoning, organisation and logical sequencing of ideas. I think engaging in this process validated Tomer's existing literacy skills and, like any initial assessment, it informed my teaching and plan for intervention.

Comment

Lisa highlights the fact that human relationships are at the heart of teaching. Teachers are not just transmitting content to students – they are engaged in a process of negotiating identities. Lisa's philosophy of attempting 'to uncover all that is unknown to me about my students' is congruent with the centrality of prior experiences and existing knowledge to all learning (Bransford, Brown and Cocking, 2000). This principle implies that teachers should seek to activate students' knowledge and explicitly teach for transfer of concepts and skills from L1 to English. When the classroom becomes an 'English-only zone', much of students' existing knowledge is, unfortunately, likely to be banished from the classroom along with their home language.

As noted in Chapter 1, the research literature on bilingual academic development shows significant relationships between literacy skills in L1 and L2. As Lisa points out, since this process of cross-linguistic transfer is happening anyway, it makes sense for teachers to encourage it and make the process efficient rather than haphazard.

Because their prior experiences and their academic abilities are encoded in their L1, teachers can gain considerable insight into students' current academic level when they encourage them to use their L1 for reading and writing tasks. Lisa notes that even when the teacher does not know a student's L1, valuable information can be gained from observation of the way the student carries out these tasks. And with a little imagination and effort, it is usually possible to find community members or other teachers and/or support personnel who can translate what students have written into English. This then sets the stage for even newcomer students to author dual language books.

Students' Experience of Bilingual Instructional Strategies
Identity affirmation and expansion
Kanta: My first language is Punjabi, my second language is Urdu, and my third language is English. Madiha had come just about a month before Ms. Leoni told us to do the story so we were just talking about the difficulties she faced and the difficulties we had faced, since we were immigrants also. Then we started talking about why not write about the differences between one country and the other, about all our differences, what was going through me when I came here, what Sulmana saw when she came here and how it was for Madiha, so that's how we came up with the idea to write the story about our three experiences.

How it helped me was when I came here in Grade 4 the teachers didn't know what I was capable of. I was given a pack of crayons and a colouring book and told to get on colouring with it. And after I felt so bad about that—I'm capable of doing much more than just that. I have my own inner skills to show the world than just coloring and I felt that those skills of mine are important also. So when we started writing the book [*The New Country*], I could actually show the world that I am something instead of just coloring. And that's how it helped me and it made me so proud of myself that I am actually capable of doing something, and here today [at the Ontario TESL conference] I *am* actually doing something. I'm not just a coloring person – I can show you that I am something.

As soon as I went home I told my parents: 'My teacher's asking us to do something in Urdu and English' and they were like 'Wow you have a chance to do something in Urdu and English, you've never had a chance to do that before!' and they were like, 'If you've got that chance, take it and go forward with it and make the best ability because we know how you felt when you were new and you didn't get that chance and now that you have the chance make it the best you can to show those other people that you're something, not just someone who has to do only coloring. So then my parents were really happy and would help me with whatever I wanted help with and they supported me.

Sulmana: When we were working on *The New Country* I felt really good and I wanted to write more stories afterward. When I was doing it I was really happy. It was fun to be able to write in both languages and to work on a project with my friends and I really liked having the chance to write in both languages and to improve my Urdu. It was my first experience translating English to Urdu so we worked together because I had forgotten many of the words in the last three years so my vocabulary improved a lot too. I had to ask my Mom a lot of words when we were writing it in Urdu but also before that, when I realised that we were going to be writing it in both languages I went home from that day and started reading more books in Urdu at home because I hadn't been doing that so much, so I had forgotten some words and I wanted my writing to make sense.

When I told my parents about the book they were really surprised to hear that their daughter could actually write in both languages and they were really happy to know that I as a normal girl who had been in Canada for the last three years actually got an opportunity to write a book in English and Urdu because when you are living in Canada you don't often get a chance to write something in Urdu or your first language.

When my grandma came here last Sunday and I told her about the book, first of all she couldn't believe it and then I said 'Wait grandma, I'll show you proof.' And I showed her the package Sarah gave us [to come to the conference]. She was so surprised and so happy that her granddaughter is so popular, that her books are all around Canada and after she saw the whole thing she was like 'Wow, you're great,' and she started kissing me.

Madiha: I write in Urdu so the Urdu people can understand, like Pakistani and Indian people who don't understand English, that's why I write Urdu. And also so my Mom can read my book because she doesn't understand English, so I write in Urdu so she can understand it too. And I like to write in Urdu because I don't want to forget my own language from my home country.

I am proud of *The New Country* because it is our story. Nobody else has written that story. And when we showed it to Ms. Leoni she said it was really good. She said 'It's about your home country, and family, and Canada, it's all connected, that's so good.' I like that because it means she cares about our family and our country, not just Canada. Because she cares about us, that makes us want to do more work. My parents were really happy to see that I was writing in both Urdu and English; my mother was happy because she knows that not everyone has that chance.

Tomer: I felt great seeing my book on the Internet because everybody could see it and I don't need to show it to everybody, they can just click on my name in Google and go to the book. I told Tom [Tomer's friend in Israel] to see it and all of my family saw it.

Tomer's mother attended the TESL Ontario session where we initially presented these findings. Her comments add weight to the impact of dual language writing – and Lisa's teaching practice generally – on both the students' sense of self and relations within the family:

> I want to say as a mother of a child in this program, we are very grateful to have a child at this school. ... The respect they have here for the child's first language is something like accepting the child. A lot of people, even teachers from this school, told us about the first two years in Canada. It was like bringing a child into a war [zone]. Two years of children nagging you and bothering you about your accent, about your manners, and about your clothes, and whatever. Our children never suffered from those things. From day one they were accepted. Their language was very respected and we are most ... I don't have the words to say it ... but we really want to thank everybody.

Teaching for Transfer

Tomer: With *Tom Goes to Kentucky* it was easier to begin it in Hebrew and then translate it to English and the other thing that made it easier was that I chose the topic. Because I love horses, when I'm writing about horses it makes me want to continue to do it and do it faster.

I think using your first language is so helpful because when you don't understand something after you've just come here it is like beginning as a baby. You don't know English and you need to learn it all from the beginning; but if you already have it in another language then it is easier, you can translate it, and you can do it in your language too, then it is easier to understand the second language.

It helps when you want to understand something but you can't and so you try to understand it in the first language and it's coming really slow and you try to translate it into English and then slowly you can get it and you can begin to ask questions and then you don't need any more the first language.

It makes it more faster to be able to use both languages instead of just breaking your head to think of the word in English when you already know the word in the other language so it makes it faster and easier to understand.

My family said it is good because then I can practice my second language and my first language and not forget it. They told me it's better when you know the first and the second language because then there are no mistakes and misunderstandings in the book.

The first time I couldn't understand what she [Lisa] was saying except the word Hebrew, but I think it's very smart that she said for us to do it in our language because we can't just sit on our hands doing nothing.

Madiha: I think it helps my learning to be able to write in both languages because if I'm writing English and Ms. Leoni says you can write Urdu too it helps me think of what the word means because I always think in Urdu. That helps me write better in English. When I came here I didn't know any English, I always speak Urdu to my friends. Other teachers they said to me 'Speak English, speak English' but Ms. Leoni didn't say anything when she heard me speak Urdu and I liked this because if I don't know English, what can I do? It helps me a lot to be able to speak Urdu and English.

Kanta: It helped me a lot to be able to write it in two languages and especially for Madiha who was just beginning to learn English because the structure of the two languages is so different. So if you want to say something in Urdu it might take just three words but in English to say the same thing you'd have to use more words. So for Madiha it helped the differences between the two languages become clear.

When I came here I was forced to speak English; I wasn't allowed to speak Urdu. So the teacher at first she gave me a coloring book and a big package of colors. From that experience of being forced to use English only, I did learn English pretty fast and it was a good thing to learn English but my English writing structure was really poor because I couldn't see the difference between Urdu and English and the process of writing them. So in one way it helped me learn English faster but for Madiha who got a chance to use both English and Urdu it helped her see the differences between the two languages and her writing in English improved a lot more and better than mine did.

Sulmana: The roles that each of us took came about pretty naturally, like Kanta was really good at translating so she did that and I was good at writing in Urdu so I did that and Madiha helped me with the vocabulary and the grammar in Urdu.

Comment

The insights of Kanta, Madiha, Sulmana and Tomer reinforce the claim that incorporation of the home language into instruction affirms students' identities and motivates them to engage with literacy in a sustained way. Sulmana also notes that the project motivated her to seek help from her Mom with Urdu words and to read more books in Urdu at home because she realised she was beginning to forget words in the language.

The students also highlight the process of cross-language transfer of knowledge and skills. Both Madiha and Tomer show the logic of enabling newcomer students to use the cognitive tools they bring to the classroom. Madiha notes: *'If I don't know English, what can I do?'* while Tomer says *'It's very smart that she said for us to do it in our language because we can't just sit on our hands doing nothing.'*

Figure 3.2: Madiha's responses to questions about use of the home language

Tomer and Madiha elaborated on the process of cross-language transfer in a written response to three questions:

- When you are allowed to write stories in class using your first language or home language, how do you feel?
- Do you enjoy reading your stories in your first/home language? Why or why not?
- When you are allowed to use your first language in class, does it help you with your writing and reading of English?

Their responses are shown in Figures 3.2 and 3.3.

Other students in Lisa's class similarly attest to the role that their home languages played in their attempts to make English comprehensible. For example Aminah says (original spelling):

> When I am allowed to use my first language in class it helps me with my writing and reading of english because if I translation in english to urdu then urdu give

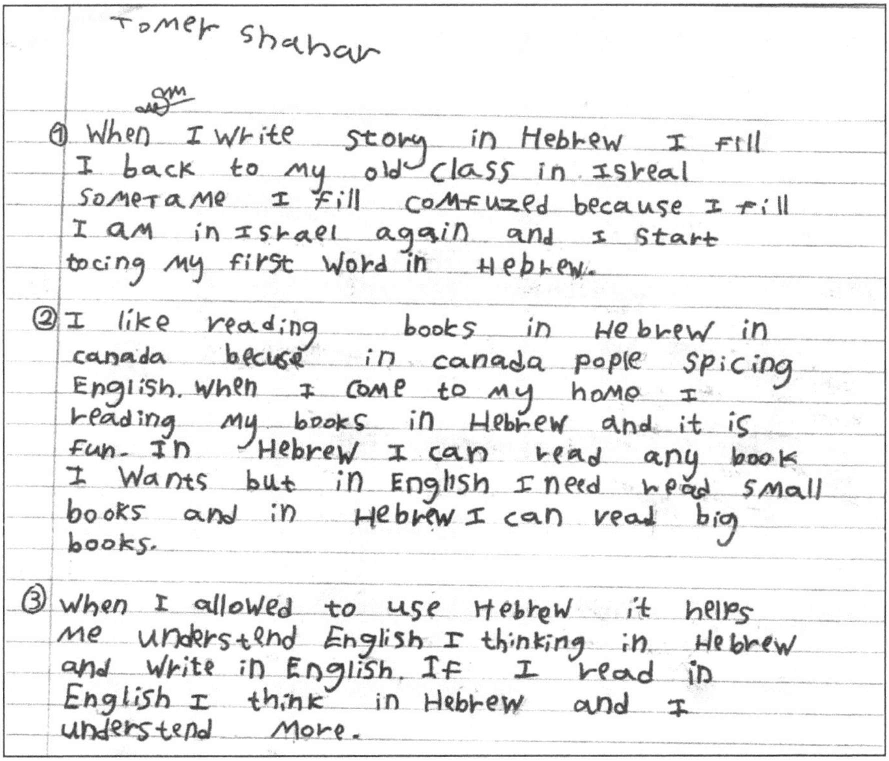

Tomer Shahar

① When I write story in Hebrew I Fill
I back to my old class in Isreal
Sometame I Fill comfuzed because I Fill
I am in Iskael again and I Start
tocing my first word in Hebrew.

② I like reading books in Hebrew in
canada becuse in canada pople spicing
English. when I come to my home I
reading my books in Hebrew and it is
fun. In Hebrew I can read any book
I wants but in English I need read small
books and in Hebrew I can read big
books.

③ When I allowed to use Hebrew it helps
me understend English I thinking in Hebrew
and write in English. If I read in
English I think in Hebrew and I
understend More.

Figure 3.3: Tomer's responses to questions about use of the home language

me help for english language. I also think better and write more in english when I use urdu because I can see in urdu what I want to say in english.

Hira elaborated on this issue as follows:

When I am allowed to use Urdu in class it helps me because when I write in Urdu and then I look at Urdu words and English comes in my mind. So, its help me a lot. When I write in English, Urdu comes in my mind. When I read in English I say it in Urdu in my mind. When I read in Urdu I feel very comfortable because I can understand it.

Conclusion

This chapter documents the impact of adopting bilingual instructional strategies in teaching emergent bilingual students. Students created dual language books and posted them on the Internet. New arrivals who spoke minimal English were enabled to participate actively in instruction and demonstrate their competent L1 literacy skills through writing in their L1. Parents and grandparents assumed new roles in their children's education in support of their children's L1 writing.

The classroom interactions documented in this case study construct a very different image of the student than the image constructed in more typical classrooms. Students were enabled to express them*selves* – their experience, intelligence, and imagination – in ways that are simply not possible when the classroom is an English-only zone. They were also enabled to use their L1 as a powerful tool for learning. The focus was on teaching for transfer rather than ignoring students' pre-existing knowledge.

The case study also illustrates the fact that language policies, which are usually implicit rather than explicit, operate within every classroom and within every school. We can explicate these policies and carry out an informal pedagogical inquiry by asking what image of the student is constructed by the (implicit or explicit) language policy of the school. Does the language policy construct an image of the student as intelligent, imaginative, and linguistically talented? Does our pedagogy acknowledge and build on the cultural and linguistic knowledge (social capital) of students and communities? To what extent are we enabling all students to engage cognitively and invest their identities in learning? Do our strategies for teaching literacy make students feel 'very comfortable, very special and very important' in the way that Madiha felt when she was given the opportunity and encouragement to write in Urdu?

Epilogue

In November 2010, Tomer, now in his last year of secondary school, was invited to sit on a panel of students at the York Regional District School Board's annual professional development conference to discuss issues related to resilience and overcoming challenges to achievement. In his presentation to participating teachers and other educators, he talks initially about how he was made to feel 'like an ESL student' in his mainstream classroom when he first arrived. But his experience was totally different as a student in Lisa's ESL classroom, where he 'gained confidence in his voice':

> In my ESL, I was given the most amazing opportunities. My teacher, Lisa Leoni ... in her classroom I did not feel like an ESL student. All it was, it was a class to develop your English, not that you are a second class student [or] that you need to learn a whole process of the Canadian ways of school. You have the knowledge, you have everything, all you need is to translate it into a different language. With her learning, I got the basis of English which let me get out of the classroom and use my assets in terms of joining boys on teams where I had very little English in the beginning but I joined the track and field team and represented my school in the regional [championships] and I had no fear of my English. I know that until now I still have an accent, I miss a couple of words here and there, but the confidence that she gave me in the first month or two in her classroom, I still use to this day – that it's OK to miss a couple of words here and there but you use the English to support you in all the other skills that I have whether it's athletics, mathematics or sciences. She gave me the confidence to use my voice, and from that ability to use my voice, I use that as a tool in everything else in the world. So I was fortunate enough to be given excellent opportunities that I don't think everyone gets.

> How did it make me feel? Gratitude ... I'm thankful for that one teacher that helped me prevail over what some people consider 'at risk', not having any English, but she helped me climb over that step and then everything from that point on was straightforward. There was no lagging behind, no nothing. ...

> The English is not a problem anymore. It's second nature almost. ... The confidence the teacher gives you, it's less the teaching, it's the confidence you get to be able to push yourself forward in the learning. It really comes down to the teachers I think. (http://wm.stream.yrdsb.ca/lrs/Quest/2010/C03Zero.wmv)

PART TWO
THE CASE STUDIES

4
Case Studies of Identity Text Creation

Introduction

We have not imposed any thematic organisation on the case studies presented in this chapter – we thought about it but decided it would be futile and largely arbitrary. So they are organised in alphabetical order according to the name of the first author of each study.

The Canadian case studies derive predominantly from two projects: the Multiliteracies project (www.multiliteracies.ca) and, to a lesser extent, the Engaging Literacies project (www.oise.utoronto.ca/lar) which followed it. Both were inspired by remarkable and innovative work that we had witnessed teachers engage in for over thirty years, linking home and school literacies and drawing on students' multiple linguistic and semiotic resources. One such project that capitalised on the affordances of technology was the Dual Language Showcase (http://thornwoodps.dyndns.org/dual/index.htm) initiated by Patricia Chow at Thornwood Public School in the Peel District School Board near Toronto (Schecter and Cummins 2003). The Dual Language Showcase also influenced a 2006 school-wide project at Hawthorne Public School (K to grade 8) in the Ottawa Carleton District School Board in which students wrote almost 500 stories in 48 languages (http://www.haw thorneps.ocdsb.ca/HawthorneWrites/index.htm). A selection of 70 stories in 28 languages was published as a book (Fuchigami, Newton and Kopczewski, 2006).

The Dual Language Showcase thus represents a powerful example of the knowledge mobilisation principle we discussed in Chapter 1 – *actuality implies possibility*. The fact that primary school children from multilingual backgrounds were able to create so many vibrant dual language texts showed that children's multilingual talents could be harnessed as a learning resource within the classroom. Our hope is that the case studies described in this chapter will continue this process of knowledge mobilisation and lead to further classroom innovation.

Case Study 1
Performing Identity Texts:
A multilingual creative writing class
in the State Prison of Oaxaca, Mexico

Angeles Clemente, Michael Higgins,
Donald Kissinger and William Sughrua

Introduction

How do inmates deal with their incarceration in the state prisons of Mexico? We explore this question in our ongoing ethnographic project based on a creative writing class that we have been teaching at a state prison in Oaxaca, the capital city of the state of Oaxaca, Mexico. This class allows the inmate-students to 'write' their way through their incarceration and thereby locate their identities momentarily beyond the walls of their confinement. We think of this as a 'liberating' activity, as illustrated in the inmate-students' bilingual/multilingual poetry (Clemente and Higgins, 2010).

Context

On the outskirts of Oaxaca is the Ixcotel state prison where we teach the creative writing class to seven inmates (two women and five men) who are incarcerated on charges ranging from the theft of car radios to homicide. Two of them have university degrees; three have high school diplomas; and the other two have not studied beyond secondary school. Although the inmate-students differ in age, previous occupations, ethnicity, and regional backgrounds, they all lack the monetary and legal resources with which to address their incarceration.

We work with the students in writing poetry. Some poems are monolingual in Spanish; others are bilingual in Spanish and English; and yet others, multilingual in Spanish, English, and Zapotec.

Process

Angeles first teaches the students to develop word clusters. From isolated words (eg *eating, pain*) the students make clusters and then transform them into poems. Angeles transcribes the poems on the computer; makes some changes, while being careful not to alter the content; scans the original and places it alongside her version on one page; and then presents this page to the students. She then engages the students in discussions about the two versions. Since the poems often deal with emotional themes (love, companionship, sensuality and betrayal) the students have become comfortable sharing their feelings and concerns.

Donald has gradually taken over the class from Angeles. He has added an English class, while continuing the creative writing class. He follows the clustering method, the only difference being that he encourages the students to use words in different languages. The students' first attempts were poems in Spanish which they haphazardly translated into English or Zapotec with the help of a dictionary. Although the students readily joke around using English and Zapotec, most of them resist using languages other than Spanish in their poems. Consequently, Donald types each poem into the computer 'as is', and then he creates an alternative version by inserting a selective number of items in English or Zapotec, taking into account sound, rhythm, appropriateness, and general usefulness. Student reaction has been polite, but the students obviously, if to different degrees, prefer their original versions. Donald and the students are caught up in on-going discussions of this resistance and its relation to issues of identity. For example, one student used exactly three English words in his poem entitled 'Gringos', and in so doing, reflected both his resistance and his identity: 'Yanqui go home!'

Output

While discussing why they rejected multilingual poetry in one of the class sessions on multilingual poems, the students came across the topic of the gringos, that is, the 'native English speakers' from the USA who come to Mexico. The students' subsequent poems on this topic touched on different sentiments and experiences, but all expressed resentment towards what the gringo figure represents for the inmate-students. Ivan's poem is a good example.

When Ivan finished reading his poem, everybody commented, saying how much they enjoyed it. They were in agreement with the juxtapositions and the use of 'gringo' as a term of endearment. They especially enjoyed the fact that Spanish is not an easy language for internationals. They even reminded

Al Gringo	To the Gringo
Tú eres del país más rico económicamente,	In terms of economy, you are from the richest country,
Pero yo soy más rico en el amor.	But I am richer in love.
Tienes toda la gran tecnología,	You have the best technology,
Pero en tu tierra nadie duerme a gusto.	But in your country nobody sleeps soundly.
En mi choza, aunque sea de cartón	In my shack, made out of cardboard,
Duermo sin preocupación.	I sleep with no worries.
Gringo le digo de cariño	I call you 'gringo' with endearment,
A aquel güero que se topo en mi camino.	You, the fair-skinned guy who has crossed my path.
Me gusta oír decir tu español mal usado.	I like to listen to your bad Spanish.
Cuando dices 'una mapa', hasta reír me haces.	When you say 'una mapa,' you even make me laugh.
Tú que vienes a explorar mi mundo	You that come to explore my world
Yo te digo que aprendas mi forma de vivir.	I tell you to learn my way of living.
No te digo gringo por joder.	I do not say 'gringo' to fuck with you.
Al contrario te lo digo con respeto,	Actually I say it with respect,
Y algún día te espero para aprender.	And one day, I expect you to learn.

Donald of when, in a previous class, he had said 'una poema'. This was a good discussion because it took some pressure off the students' own learning of English.

Impact

The creative writing class has had a great impact within the context of the prison. The seven inmate-students in the class have composed over 150 poems and have generated a great deal of interest within the Ixcotel prison community. This has generated four poetry readings, participation in a national poetry contest for prisoners, and the continuation of the creative writing class. There are also plans to send the inmate-students' poems to national and international journals and even to put together an anthology of their writings including our comments. José, one of the students, hopes that people outside start thinking about him and his classmates 'as human beings worth knowing about and not as human debris' (Clemente and Higgins, 2010).

The process itself is also important for the inmate-students. On several occasions they have said that the writing course creates a 'therapeutic atmosphere' (Miguel) and 'a space where we feel we are not incarcerated' (Paco) and 'where we can share and explore our feelings' (Jorge). The atmosphere of the course is very relaxing. The students speak freely. They talk about events in the prison and make jokes about each other and even about us. This last, for instance, was one of the recurrent themes in the 'gringo' poems such as Ivan's above: 'When you say 'una mapa', you even make me laugh.'

In this manner, the inmate-students are social actors, utilising their poems as localised forms of cultural literacy practices. They challenge the issue of who gets to validate what is or is not literacy; they stake a claim to the value of their localised knowledge production; and they imagine something beyond their immediate situation (Mignolo, 2001). Hence by envisioning the possibility of alternative futures, they subvert the attempt to mark their hopes and sentiments as short term and unrealistic, and thus exercise their identity (Dussel, 2002). They are able to affirm these liberating activities through a praxis of literacy (writing poems) that allows them to express their new or imagined identities beyond the prison walls (Kanno and Norton, 2003; Purcell-Gates, 2007).

References

Clemente, A and Higgins, M (2010) 'Prison break': La praxis de las performancias lingüísticas en la prisión estatal de Oaxaca, Mexico. Conferencia presentada en el *Encuentro Académico sobre Prácticas Culturales en el Lenguaje Oral y Escrito*, Universidad Autónoma 'Benito Juárez' de Oaxaca, Oaxaca, Mexico, Enero 2010

Dussel, E (2002) World-system and 'trans'-modernity. *Nepantla: Views from South*, 3(2), p221-244

Kanno, Y and Norton, B (2003) Imagined communities and educational opportunities: Introduction. *Journal of Language, Identity, and Education*, 2(4), p241-249

Mignolo, W (2001). Colonialidad del poder y subalternidad. In I. Rodriquez (ed) *Convergencia de Tiempos: Estudios subalterno/contextos latinoamericanos: Estado, cultura, subalternidad*. Amsterdam and Atlanta: Editions Rodopi B.V.

Purcell-Gates, V (2007) Complicating the Complex. In V. Purcell-Gates (ed) *Cultural Practices of Literacy: Case studies of language, literacy, social practice, and power*. Mahwah, New Jersey: Lawrence Erlbaum Associates, Inc.

Further Reading

Clemente, A and Higgins, M (2010). Performing methodological activities in postcolonial ethnographic encounters: Examples from Oaxaca, Mexico. In F Shamim and R Qureshi (eds), *Perils, Pitfalls and Reflexivity in Qualitative Research in Education*. Oxford: Oxford University Press

Clemente, A Higgins, M and Sughrua, W (2010). 'Thanks for the blanket that was lent to me the first night': Ethnographic encounters with cultural practices of literacy in the state prison of Oaxaca. Paper under review at *Language and Linguistics*

Case Study 2
Multilingual Identity Texts in the Library Curriculum
Sarah Cohen and Padma Sastri

Introduction

This is a case study of the initiatives taken by Padma, a teacher librarian in an elementary school in the Greater Toronto Area (GTA), to use her students' home languages as a resource for increasing their engagement with literacy and their development of literacy skills and concepts. The purpose of the research was to observe and document the strategies that Padma was implementing in her library curriculum that built on students' and families' multilingual resources and at the same time to support her in this process.

Context

The study took place in the GTA, where more than half the population was born outside Canada. The City of Toronto website expresses the demographic reality as follows:

> Almost three-quarters of Torontonians aged 15 or older have direct ties to immigration. About one-half (52%) are themselves immigrants while another 22 per cent are 2nd generation immigrants with at least one parent born outside of Canada. The remaining 26 per cent of the Toronto population (aged 15 or older) is comprised of individuals who were born in Canada to two Canadian-born parents. (http://www.toronto.ca/quality_of_life/diversity.htm)

These demographics are reflected in Floradale Public School, where Padma teaches. At the time of the research, Floradale had more than 700 students from Junior Kindergarten (JK, age 4) through Grade 6 who came from 88 different countries and spoke 44 different languages. The school is part of the Peel District School Board located about 20 kilometres west of downtown

Toronto. The 2005 census reported that 43 per cent of the 100,000 residents in the area had immigrated to Canada (*Globe and Mail*, 2005).

The action research was carried out in the context of the Multiliteracies project in 2003 and 2004. Padma has made the cultural and linguistic diversity that is reflected in her school population a central focus of her teaching. As the teacher librarian, she held classes with all grade levels, JK through Grade 6. The data collected as part of the action research collaboration included classroom observations, interviews with Padma and participating students, video documentation of classroom activities, and samples of student work from across the grade levels.

Process

In her teaching, Padma integrated a multilingual focus throughout the day. For example, while conducting pre-reading activities with a Kindergarten class about the counting book she was sharing (*Handa's Hens* [Browne, 2002]), Padma asked students to name what they saw two of on the pages. After several students offered responses ranging from two eyes, two hens, two eggs, two girls, one student called out: 'Two languages'.

Padma also found ways to expand on already existing literacy activities to include a multilingual component. For example, students created dual language 'flipbooks' as a reading response tool. Students wrote down their favourite parts, together with new vocabulary and filled out a graphic organiser (such as a Venn Diagram) focused on comprehension about the book they had read and then they translated this into their L1 (see Figure 4.1). Sometimes this translation required working with a parent to help them write in their L1. This created a shared literacy event with families and it also created an opportunity for parents and students to showcase their multilingual abilities. When Padma encouraged students to share these small dual language books at the school's weekly assembly, this further validated students' identities and provided a wider audience for their work.

Padma extended the readers' theatre activity she had previously done in her classes to include a multilingual element. The students either spoke the parts in a range of languages or retold the story in their L1. She encouraged students to use 'a lot of their first language and a little English or a little of their first language and a lot of English', depending on what configuration they were most comfortable with. This recognised the continuum of bilingualism that her students represented and encouraged all of them to adopt a positive attitude towards their multilingual abilities.

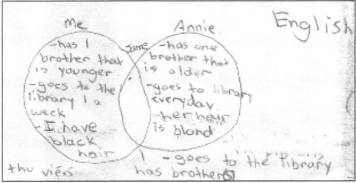

Figure 4.1: An excerpt from Jenny's Vietnamese and English flipbook. http://www.multiliteracies.ca/index.php/folio/ viewGallery Book/5/124

The vignette below from Sarah's field notes describes one such event:

Padma assembles her sari around her as she sits in her chair at the front of the rug in the library. Roughly 27 fourth grade students assemble cross-legged in front of her as she launches into the day's lesson.

'Now I need eight people to help with reading the story. Loud and clear', Padma says, as she calls two children to sit next to her. Each chooses somebody else and so on until there are four on either side of her.

'And who would like to tell the story in their language after we've heard it read?' Several students raise their hands. 'Are we ready?' she asks, 'Do we all have our listening ears? Do we have our translating tongues? Let's go. Big voices.'

The story telling begins. Padma leads the chorus in their calls of 'Oooh' when the voices go too low to be heard and 'Ah haah' when the voices are strong and loud. I feel as though I am in a theatre.

'Now', says Padma as she gestures toward the row of students seated in the chairs opposite her, 'These people are going to tell us the story in another language.'

I listen amazed as one by one I hear and see the story repeated first in Urdu, then Turkish, Vietnamese, Russian, Chinese, Gujerati, Tamil and in Korean twice and Arabic three times. The other students in the class appear as entranced as I am, though neither I, nor all of them understand most of the languages being used. It is captivating to see the same story repeated with new or sometimes the same gestures while the words that express the action change.

Impact

Students' comments highlighted the relationship between these activities and their multilingual identities. As just one example, Nava expressed the pleasure she took in this activity:

I like it because I get to know what other kids speak and some words they speak it in because we might know some of the words from them. So...you get to know other people, you get to know what languages they speak in, and more about their languages.

Nava's comments show that she likes being asked to use her L1; she also points to the link that is promoted between school and home by participating in dual language storytelling:

When I come across some words I don't know I add in the English word but when I get home I ask my parents what the word is in Urdu and they tell me and I get to know my language better.

The students in this study were able to maintain a positive attitude toward their L1, something that is not common for emergent bilinguals in many educational contexts. Padma's teaching made students' cultural and linguistic identities an integral element and a positive force within the curriculum. Nadir, in Grade 6 at the time of this study, said that when he has the chance to retell a story in his L1, Hindi, 'It feels great, I feel perfect, I feel like I'm back in India.'

References

Browne, E (2002) *Handa's Hens*. London, England: Walker Books

City of Toronto: Diversity. Retrieved August 12, 2010 from: http://www.toronto.ca/quality_of_life/diversity.htm

Globe and Mail (2005). 'Suburbs suffer inner-city ills, but little relief offered: report' p.A4. Retrieved May 14, 2005, from http://www.globeandmail.ca

Further reading

Multiliteracies website: http://www.multiliteracies.ca/index.php/folio/viewDocument/5/4843

Case Study 3
Creating Picture Books and Performance as Identity Texts in a Core French Classroom
Margaret Early and Cindy Yeung

Introduction

This case study was conducted in Vancouver, British Columbia in a Grade 9 Core French class, a French as a second language program generally taught in 50-minute periods every other day. While Canada is officially a bilingual country, it is widely known that these Core French language programs have not met with great success and the dropout rates are high. In this context and given that French is not a mandatory subject beyond Grade 8 in the province, Cindy, the teacher, determined that it was especially critical to design pedagogical tasks that her students would invest in and that would promote a desire for them to continue their learning of French. To that end, she designed a multi-stage project in which students composed original children's stories in French, illustrated their stories to produce picture books for young readers, then, in groups, adapted one group member's story into a play script. The final stage was to perform the plays for an audience of children from the local French Immersion school. The students worked across modes (linguistic, visual, dramatic and musical) and genres (picture books, scripts and performances) to construct rich and vital identity texts in French.

Context for the study

The study was conducted at Lord Byng High School, located on the west side of Vancouver. The participants in this study were: the teacher, Cindy, and 34 students in a Core French 9 'Enriched' class. The students were recommended on the strength of their achievement in French 8 (C+ or above) and a self-expressed interest in francophone language and culture. They were a lively and energetic multi-ethnic group with a range of academic ability; some students were designated as having 'learning challenges', some as 'gifted'.

The process: designing multimodal, multi-stage tasks

Stage 1: Individual authoring of stories

Because students aged 5-8 years old from the local French Immersion school were the intended audience for students' books, the class initially examined and read samples of French picture books written for this age group. This provided a natural context for a great deal of comprehensible input, interaction and output for the learners as they discussed the content and book design, in French, to the best of their ability. For the first draft of their books, the students produced much of the text and illustration in lieu of homework. They consulted with Cindy, and received feedback on request. Then they brought their completed first drafts and images to class for peer editing. Working in groups of four, each student exchanged papers with at least two others in their group. Next, they handed over their work to Cindy for feedback. The students now set about putting their work more formally in picture book format. They had artistic freedom and were encouraged to make additional edits to their texts to fit the illustrations and graphic design. On completion of the books and after a final check by Cindy, the class had a mini-gallery exhibition of their works of art in the school library. This was well attended by school and community members.

Stages 2 and 3: Adapted play script and group dramatisation of stories

The students organised themselves into groups of five to six. Each group selected one member's story to adapt into a script for dramatic presentation. In this process, narrators and, in some cases, new characters were added so that everyone had a speaking part. Working collaboratively, students practiced their skills in delegating roles and finding ways to showcase each individual's strengths. They prepared the costumes, set designs, stage directions and, in the case of two groups, musical accompaniment. Cindy invited a Grade 2/3 French Immersion class from a nearby school to come and view the performances. The school library served as the performance venue as well as gallery space to display all the picture books.

The identity text

The students clearly invested their identities, individually and collectively, in these multimodal texts, as the example in Figure 4.2 illustrates. They produced a wide range of visual designs and materiality which included computer-animated illustrations, collages of tree twigs, fabric, watercolour, metallic foil, and an intricate fold-out pop-up book 'sculpture'. There was a wide variety of genres including myths, fairy tales, fantasy, mystery, drama, humour and non-fiction.

In addition to the picture books, students created and performed six plays. These were rich dramas and melodramas which included pantomime, music, dance, and slapstick comedy. The young audience was enthralled. They cheered, yelled and applauded after each 10-15 minute drama. After the performances, the young audience members had lots of opportunity to view, read or have read to them, all the individual picture books and to interact with the Core French 9 authors and performers. The students worked hard to communicate in French across the age spans, with the young students asking many questions about the characters in the texts.

The teacher's and students' responses to the identity texts
From Cindy's perspective:

> I wanted to create a project in which I held up high standards because they [the students] are capable of so much more than we ask in the Core French classroom. I also wanted to motivate them to choose to go on and learn more French. I thought that if they could see what they could actually do in French and had a lot of fun that would be the best way. So a real audience was important. I gave a lot of freedom and I thought they would really invest, and they did. They more than lived up to my expectations.

As far as the students were concerned, one girl explained why she had worked so hard and was so invested in her identity text: 'The stories were of my preference because it was me/mine.' One of the boys told us, 'I enjoyed being able to invent characters and create villains. It was great to see my imagination put into words in another language.' Another said, 'I realised I wasn't just writing this for the students but I was writing about my interests and choices too, and because I felt like I was putting myself out there, I wanted to do a good job.'

Similar sentiments were repeatedly expressed with respect to the performances. One girl explained, 'It was challenging because you weren't sure if the audience understood or enjoyed what you were saying. We worked hard, though, to make the language clear and our pronunciation easy to understand. We felt great at the end.' At the end of the project, students completed a Likert-scale survey. Ninety-three per cent agreed or strongly agreed that

Figure 1: Picture book created by Ingrid Braul
http://www.multiliteracies.ca/index.php/folio/viewGalleryBook/19/149

they felt more confident in both writing and reading comprehension of French; 86 per cent felt more confident in their listening comprehension; and 97 per cent were more confident in their speaking skills. All said they were motivated to continue to learn French. By many measures, creating identity texts appears to have had the empowering outcomes Cindy had imagined for her students.

Further reading

Early, M and Yeung, C (2009) Producing multimodal picture books and dramatic performances in core French: An exploratory case study. *Canadian Modern Language Review*, 66(2), p299-223.

Website

http://www.multiliteracies.ca/index.php/folio/viewProject/19

Case Study 4
Weaving Other Languages and Cultures into the Curriculum in International Primary Schools
Eithne Gallagher

Introduction

English is the medium of instruction in the vast majority of International Schools but the student population of these schools is made up largely of children whose L1 is other than English. However, the fact that International Schools serve an international population does not mean that they follow an international curriculum or employ international educators who are committed to educating students in ways that make use of children's multilingual talents. In many International Schools this is simply not the case. Children are often discouraged from using their L1 within the school.

The children in International Schools are privileged in many ways. They come from affluent families; their parents are often professional people who have high expectations for their children. The schools they attend are often situated in beautiful locations and are aesthetically very pleasant places to be. They are generally overflowing with resources and have abundant libraries, spilling over with books in the English language.

Some children, especially those whose parents are part of the global mobile workforce, move and encounter a new language every few years. These 'global elitelings' can arrive as young as 3 years old in our Early Childhood classrooms. You can imagine their bewildered state as they learn nursery rhymes and listen to stories in a strange tongue; especially – as is often the case – when they find themselves with a group of children who speak the same home language as they do but are not allowed or encouraged to use it. What message are we giving children by this?

In recent years, an increasing number of educators in International Schools have been trying to articulate and implement a new plurilingual understanding of what the 'international' in International Schools should represent (see Gallagher, 2008 for an outline of these ideas). We have argued that students and teachers alike should begin to consider their classes as *interlingual*, where the *inter* stands for international-mindedness, that is, the notion that everyone should be open and responsive to learning about other languages. In interlingual classrooms teachers encourage children to make use of all their languages to help them become aware of the differences and similarities of languages. There is normally one language of instruction but all the languages in the classroom can be used to help children access it. This does require the teacher to be a polyglot, but she does need to have a mindset that is open to other languages and cultures, and to be interested in learning from both students and their families. This opportunity and mindset would, of course, also be passed on to those children in the class who speak only English.

Many enlightened ESL teachers in International Schools have been teaching for some years in ways that validate children's languages and cultures. But this perspective is not yet incorporated into most mainstream instructional contexts in International Schools. Identity text creation represents a powerful way of beginning this conversation between ESL and mainstream teachers about the value of children's home languages and cultures. The experience I describe below demonstrates how successful identity text creation can be in instilling linguistic pride in students within a mainstream classroom context.

Context

I teach children who are learning English in Marymount International School in Rome, Italy and the identity text project the class teacher and I implemented involved a class of seventeen Grade 4 children from different language backgrounds. Only one child in the group was monolingual. Nine children considered Italian to be their strongest language. The others came from Arabic, Amharic, Greek, Korean, Portuguese, Spanish and Russian backgrounds. The class teacher, Claudia De Rocchis, is a Canadian of Italian origin who, like me, speaks English, French and Italian. We had little knowledge of the other fifteen languages used in this project but we learnt much from the children and their parents as we progressed.

Our school strives to instil in our children an awareness of the world as a global community and the part we can all play in making the world a better place. One of the local charities the school is involved with is The Peter Pan

Association (http://www.peterpanonlus.it/), which helps children to become aware of the problems faced by families with children fighting to recover from cancer. The Association seeks to provide a link between the hospitalised child and the healthy child. To promote awareness of their work, they run an annual competition called The Peter Pan Project. The Grade 4 class had decided to take part in this and Claudia invited me to lead the class in some collaborative writing. The children were asked to write a story or poem for blind children based on the theme of 'Respect towards others who are different from us'. They chose to write a story.

Process

I began by discussing with the children the theme and how each child in the class was unique. Very quickly we found ourselves talking about language and cultural differences. We learned how to say 'respect' and 'accept' in all the languages of the class. We wanted the blind children to know how diverse our group was and so it was decided that we would write, collaboratively, a multilingual tale and make a CD of it in English and all the other languages so the blind children would be able to listen to the story.

Next we decided on the genre for the story; it was to be a fairytale. We discovered that fairytales in many languages begin and end the same way so we made a multilingual poster of all the different scripts representing the notions of *Once upon a time...* and *They all lived happily ever after...* and we hung this centre stage in the classroom. Each child and teacher was given a Fairytale Planner where they had to write ideas under the headings of Good Characters, Bad Characters, The Problem, The Magic and The Happy Ending. They were free to write their ideas in their L1 or in English. I then asked the children to give me all the names for the characters. I put them all on the flip chart and we voted to choose the ones we would use for the story. We then listened to each others' ideas for problems and magic and so on, and decided to get started with our story writing and make decisions about how we would proceed as we went along.

The children had plenty of opportunities for discussion and they were free to interact in their L1. The class teacher and I spoke in English but constantly asked questions like 'How do you say such-and-such in Greek, Amharic, etc.'? The atmosphere was relaxed but respectful. No one felt excluded and everyone sensed they had something to offer. I elicited and scribed, changed and crossed out, added and discussed. Some of the children wrote on the flipchart words and phrases in their L1 when they had difficulty expressing their ideas in English. They later worked with the class teacher using the translation tools available in the Google and Babel Fish web sites and wrote the English above their L1 text. We added punctuation, edited and revised, and finally we were happy with our tale. Next, we decided where the page breaks should be. Once the story was divided up each child had a page to illustrate and write their bit of the story in their L1 and in English. We invited the children to choose which part of the story they wanted to illustrate so that each child felt they had ownership.

Outcomes

Our project culminated with the production of a multilingual booklet, protected by a clear plastic cover, containing the dual language texts and illustrations the children had created. We also produced a PowerPoint presentation with integrated voiceover of the children themselves each reading their own pages. A CD copy of the book was also produced.

Other less tangible but nonetheless valid outcomes included various live presentations performed by the students for their grade peers, students visiting from other schools, and parents. The students were so enthusiastic and involved that they started a project to write a play based on their story. The illustrations in Figure 4.2 show some of the pages from our book.

Impact

When we started to discuss languages, we discovered that many of the children felt they were better readers and writers in English than they were in their L1. This was especially true for those from non-Italian backgrounds who had been in International Education for most of their school lives.

Figure 4.2: Pages from *The Power of Friendship*

The child who spoke Lebanese did not know how to read and write it (we discovered that her parents were having a hard time getting her even to respond to them in Arabic). She was learning French with her father and that was the language she wanted to use. An Italian girl whose mother was teaching her Spanish decided she wanted to write her piece in Spanish. This prompted the Argentinean boy who is trilingual in Spanish, Portuguese and English to help her with Spanish. We were rather surprised, as he had generally been one of the more reserved and timid members of the group but evidently this context gave him the opportunity to shine as a linguistic expert and he was really keen to do so. Another Italian girl wrote her text in German; her father was a fluent speaker of German and although she had no knowledge of it, she was eager to learn it.

I think it is interesting that some of the Italian children chose not to write in Italian. This perhaps shows that, since Italian is the majority language in the school, they felt more secure in their linguistic identity and therefore readier to seize the opportunity to investigate other languages. It also demonstrates how this kind of exercise gives children a hunger to know more about different languages. The children who came from bilingual families (Italian and another language) chose the other language.

All the children needed help from their parents to write and to practise reading their texts. Several children, although fluent in their L1 (Arabic, Amharic and Russian), did not know how to read or write it well. The Italian children were competent readers and writers of Italian, as they had been receiving formal instruction in school in Italian since first grade. The Greek boy, too, could read and write Greek well. He had only been at the school for a year and his parents had been encouraged from day one to maintain his home language. The Korean girl, who had grown up in Italy and is trilingual, chose to write in Korean; although a fluent speaker, she too needed help from her parents. The monolingual American girl had been learning Italian in school for a couple of years. She did not like Italian and did not want to try and write her text in it. When I talked with her, I discovered she wanted to learn Dutch. Her best friend came from Holland. She had been at the school but had returned to Amsterdam. I told her to e-mail her and ask her to translate the text. When this was done I found an older Dutch student to help the child with reading the translation.

After the book had been created, the next phase involved turning the classroom into a recording studio. Before doing the final recording, we invited other classes to come and listen to the tale and follow a PowerPoint presentation of the book. Our good and bad characters looked a little different on each page as each child had a different notion of what a fairy and a dragon looked like. Every single child was immensely proud of the book. I cannot tell you how many times children would stop me in the corridor to ask 'When are you coming to work on our book?' The class teacher (Claudia) had the good idea of making copies of the CD and book to sell to raise money for our sister school in Zambia. Grandparents, aunts, uncles and friends of Grade 4 all over the globe received copies of our multilingual tale, *The Power of Friendship*.

In Claudia's words:

> The Power of Friendship promoted inquiry and respectful communication among the languages, cultures and religions within our classroom community. Working together as a group through the reading, writing and recording process, the 4th Graders were engaged and continuously interacting in different languages as they built trust, compromise and encouragement with each other. Their enthusiasm to share their own language and to learn other languages and their passion for wanting to make a difference in the life of other people was the key to such a creative and moving project which generated a positive and memorable learning atmosphere. This project made me realise how important encouraging children to think and use not only their own languages but listen to other languages is for building a better community and a better world.

I firmly believe that knowing another language helps people see the world afresh. Our world needs to be seen and understood in a new way. Using identity texts in school helps create an awareness of other languages, whilst at the same time strengthening the inner identity of the child that all too often goes unnoticed in International Schools, where the main focus is on accelerating English language growth.

Reference
Gallagher, E (2008) *Equal Rights to the Curriculum: Many languages, one message*. Clevedon: Multilingual Matters

Further reading/viewing
The Power of Friendship book can be viewed and heard at the following sites: www.marymount rome.org http://www.youtube.com/watch?v=fb68Ob9QQg4

An outline of the pedagogical approach from the perspective of multilingual students can be viewed at: http://www.youtube.com/watch?v=-tFA0IPeSjU&feature=related

Case Study 5
'We're just like real authors':
The power of dual language identity texts in a multilingual school

Frances Giampapa and Perminder Sandhu

Introduction

This case study describes how Perminder drew upon her own multilingual, multicultural and racial identities and those of her students in developing a multiliteracies pedagogy within her classroom. In the initial year of the project (2003/2004), Perminder's students worked in pairs to create dual language stories, often with help from parents and other family members. In the second year (2004/2005), grade 4 and grade 7 students collaborated in creating dual language books.

The case study was part of the broader Multiliteracies project described in Chapter 1. The collaboration between the university-based researcher (Frances) and the school-based researcher (Perminder) was designed to address two questions:

- In what ways can teachers' own linguistic and cultural experiences provide a pedagogical base for understanding their students' funds of knowledge?
- In what ways can students' L1 and cultural knowledge be incorporated into the English-medium curriculum and provide a broader base for (bi)literacy engagement?

The project took place in Coppard Glen Public School, which is situated in the Greater Toronto Area. In recent years, the demographic of this school has changed considerably, with a significant increase in new immigrants from India, Pakistan, Sri Lanka and China.

Process

Teachers at Coppard Glen who were interested in being involved in the Multi-literacies project formed a 'Multiliteracies Committee' which met at regular intervals to discuss issues of language and culture at the school and initiatives they were pursuing in their classrooms. Twelve of the more than 40 teachers in the school served on this committee.

The committee decided to start by exploring and writing about their own linguistic and cultural experiences, how these experiences connected to their students' experiences, and what this in turn means for their teaching. Many had themselves endured shame and marginalisation in relation to their language and culture in the educational context. This is poignantly captured in one teacher's reflection:

> As a student, I remember only too vividly the trauma of walking into a class where I didn't understand much of what went on, of being very afraid, bewildered and de-skilled. My rich resource of my first language accumulated over 13 years had suddenly been rendered redundant. Children in these situations are left to sink or swim. I do not want that to happen to my students in my class or in my school. http://www.multiliteracies.ca/index.php/folio/viewGallery SlideShow/38/564

Discussions within the Multiliteracies Committee enabled many of these teachers to reconnect with their own feelings of disempowerment when they, as students, were made to leave their own identities and home languages at the schoolhouse door. These memories were a driving force in their impulse to find ways to value their students' linguistic and cultural capital, and to use it as a pedagogical resource.

The teachers asked students in different grade levels to reflect on their home languages and write about how they would feel about using them in school. When the teachers met to discuss the students' responses, they were surprised by how many had expressed reservations or nervousness about the legitimacy of using their L1 in the school context. A number of them expressed pride in their L1 but felt that it would not be permissible to use L1 in the school context. One grade 4 student put it like this:

> I feel that when I speak my first language I will be accepted not rejected. If I had the permission to speak my first language, I will feel confident, free, feel like I can catch a dream and run with it.

Over the course of the project, Perminder and other teachers shared their own linguistic experiences and competences with their students and initiated whole class discussions that built up students' awareness of the value of languages and diversity in general. The creation of identity texts was a concrete realisation of the power of languages to amplify students' identities.

Creating dual language identity texts

The grade 4 project

In the initial dual language project conducted in Perminder's class, students were encouraged to self-select book themes, to work in pairs and write in the languages of their choice. The L1 literacies and abilities of her students varied and not all pairs of students had the same L1. Students worked collaboratively in composing, editing, and visually representing their words through hand drawn pictures and/or digital art.

Perminder based the student pairings on students' social-emotional levels and their literate abilities in their L1 and English. This was the first time that students had been actively engaged in multiliterate practices in both their languages. Those who had believed that their L1 had no place within the school were now working with multilingual dictionaries and drawing on their families' cultural and linguistic competences and knowledge to create in some cases lengthy dual language books. Translation between languages and metalinguistic talk about language was integral to this process.

One of the books created as part of the dual language text project was *The Hook* (Figure 4.4), jointly created by Jananan and Sunny. Jananan's home language was Tamil, Sunny's Punjabi. Jananan describes the process of creating the book:

> First like there was 12 pages of the story. Me and Sunny took six separate pages each... We composed the story together. We decided to do the story in Tamil and I would do it on my computer at home and then Sunny would write again in his language...we would have two copies one in English and Tamil, one in English and Punjabi.

The grade 4/7 collaboration

The success of the initial project was replicated in a cross-grade class collaboration between grade 4 and grade 7 students in 2004/2005. Jo-Anne, a grade 7 teacher, and Perminder brought their classes together to enable their students to jointly create dual language books. Jo-Anne noted that she was intrigued by Perminder's work with her students and by the dual language texts they produced. She declared that when the Multiliteracies Committee discussed potential projects for the following year, 'My eyes lit up and I thought, let's try the writing buddies and do a dual text'.

Figure 4.4: A page from *The Hook*

The teachers provided story guidelines through overt instruction, and students co-created and negotiated stories with their cross-grade partners. Jo-Anne and Perminder discussed with students the following guidelines to scaffold the writing of their stories:

- genre
- characters
- setting
- introductory hook
- languages of the text
- conflict
- key events
- problem and resolution

- ▨ style of materials – layout of the text and illustrations
- ▨ dedication.

These guidelines are consistent with the Ontario Language Arts curriculum for both these grade levels. The students learned together how to write for a particular audience, to peer-edit using technology, to provide feedback to other student partners, and to collaboratively create the layout and artwork to accompany their texts. Students did not always share the same home language, so texts were created in multiple languages.

The identity investment that book authoring can generate is captured by Arshia, a grade 4 student, and Vasko, a grade 7 student, who were producing a multilingual story entitled 'Around the World in 80 days'. They were responding to a question about what was special about the process:

> Vasko: Just the whole idea of ... making a book.
>
> Arshia: Yeah, like publishing it.
>
> Vasko: publishing it.
>
> Arshia: It's almost like we're like authors but except younger. Because authors are usually ... most of them are like grown-ups and stuff. Important as if like we're actually *real* authors ourselves and making a book. ... For the books that the grade 4s did last year I did a picture for them. And it was fun to go see my picture on the Internet. ... Also I think, I thought it was kinda a good idea making it in different languages because since like it's going to be on the Internet and stuff then maybe the grandparents or parents can read it and tell like other people.

The centrality of teacher identity

Perminder's transformative pedagogy was fuelled by her own multiple identities and the politics around her self-positioning as a Black woman and a member of a cultural and religious minority group. She was born in India, raised in the United Kingdom, and at the time of the project had been living in Canada for around eight years. She is multilingual and of Sikh background. She wrote:

> Who am I? I guess I am an Indo-British Canadian and a global citizen. My reality is shaped significantly by my own world-view, in which power dynamics play a significant role. My identity is impacted also by my linguistic, cultural, social, political and spiritual experiences. Living as a member of the minority community, and as a black woman, my identity is inevitably linked with how the majority members view me. I see my evolving identity as my responsibility,

which I need to nurture, protect, strengthen, challenge, and indulge. As we recognise multiple facets of our own identity, and move away from the simplistic notions of cultural identifications, I believe that we are better able to foster the development of our students' multiple identities. The interplay of how we identify ourselves, and how the world identifies us, is crucial for our own evolving identity.

The power of Perminder's pedagogy lies in the connection it makes to students' identities, knowledges and multiliteracies. The dual language identity texts created the possibility for students to be heard, valued and recognised.

Further reading
Giampapa, F (2010) Multiliteracies, pedagogy and identities: teacher and student voices from a Toronto elementary school'. *Canadian Journal of Education*, 33(2) p407-431.

Website
http://www.multiliteracies.ca/index.php/folio/viewDocument/38/11470

Case Study 6
Identity Journals in Multicultural/ Multilingual Schools in Greece

Vasilia Kourtis-Kazoullis

Introduction

In education, the journal has often been used as a means to foster creative writing in L1 instruction. However, it can also be used in L2 instruction. Diaries/journals have been used to promote metalinguistic reflection among second language learners and as a means of language exploration. Ungraded and uncorrected journals can be utilised in ESL classes as they can provide a non-threatening way for students to express themselves. New technologies have created a new form of journal with a potentially unlimited audience, namely blogs. These have been used to improve the written language of native speakers as well as second language learners.

The Identity Journal is a book in which students can use the target language or any other language in their language repertoire to express their identities and interests. Thus it is a collection of identity texts, within the realm of a trans-formative model of pedagogy (see Chapter 2). Transformative approaches to pedagogy promote critical literacy among students, to enable them to analyse societal discourses and conceptualise forms of action so they can affect them (Skourtou, Kourtis-Kazoullis and Cummins, 2006). Figure 4.5 outlines the theoretical basis of Identity Journals.

In the Identity Journal, language is used to explore and express identity and interests, to create literature and art, to critically examine social realities, and to express opinions, emotions and feelings. It combines maximum identity investment, intrinsic motivation, maximum cognitive involvement and critical literacy, as students express themselves through identity texts and criti-cally examine realities relevant to their lives. Their identity is viewed positively.

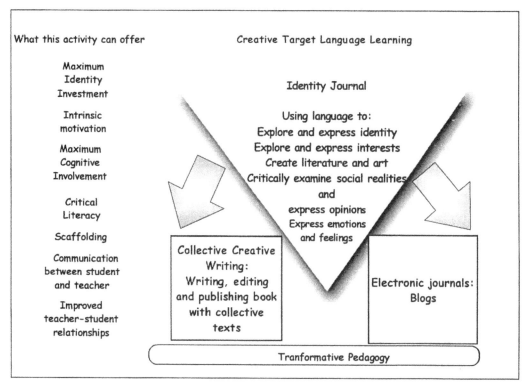

Figure 4.5: Theoretical basis of Identity Journals

Scaffolding is provided through dialogue (oral and written) between student and teacher. As learning becomes more personal, teacher-student relationships are improved.

In the project described in this case study, students wrote in their own Identity Journals but shared their texts with multiple audiences in the following ways:

- Texts were shared in class with other students, giving others ideas and inspiration; the texts also served as a source of discussion and critical analysis of social issues
- Texts from the journals were published as one collective volume (in this case, they were published in a book, but they can also be published on the Internet)
- The book transforms students into authors and experts and this status was reinforced when the student authors themselves presented a seminar on identity to the entire school and then to all the teachers in the city, thereby offering teachers new pedagogical ideas and insights.

Context

Nine classes in grades 10, 11, and 12 in a Senior High School on one of the Greek islands participated in the Identity Journal writing project as part of their English lessons. English as a foreign language (EFL) lessons in the school provided 'neutral' ground for the project as all the students, whatever their Greek language proficiency, were language learners. The school was characterised by cultural and linguistic diversity, many of the students were from culturally mixed families, immigrants from other countries or migrants from other parts of the country, or they commuted to the school every day from nearby villages. The school was in an area of the city characterised by government housing and low-income families. Greek schools have a common national curriculum and the curriculum focuses on drilling students for college entrance exams, especially in senior high school. Consequently, activities that stray away from the national curriculum are not common.

Process

Each student chose to use a hardcover book with blank pages rather than a typical high school notebook. It was important that the students had the impression that they were writing their own book and not just an ordinary assignment. The EFL teacher introduced journal writing to the students by explaining what a journal is, giving examples of famous journals and instructions on how to write a journal. Most of the students had never written in a journal before, especially not in school. The first entry they were asked to write was a personal profile. Students were encouraged to provide pictures of themselves, past and present. Those who were less skilled in English writing were given additional support in the form of a guided writing frame.

Provided with a data bank of creative writing ideas and through brainstorming in class, the students collectively thought of other ideas for creative writing, and these ideas were shared with the other classes. Once a week the students brought their journal to class and the EFL teacher suggested topics the students could write about in class or at home. The teacher or students also brought material in the form of visual or audio aids, such as pictures, magazines, CDs, in the target language. Students could choose one of the topics, but were encouraged to find topics that personally interested them. If something caught their attention during the week – a news event, newspaper article, picture, song, video, etc – they were encouraged to keep it in a special folder they could use later as an inspiration data bank and share with others. They were encouraged to use multimodal forms of inspiration and to keep multimodal journals. The journals began in traditional book form but were expanded by many students to include CDs of music they had composed and performed themselves, and other electronic forms of expression.

As well as time dedicated to journal writing in class, the students were encouraged to write in their journals during their free time. They were also allowed to do so at any time during classroom time when the lesson in progress did not interest them. This was very important as the foreign language classes in public education are often mixed ability, so the journal allowed students who were at a higher level to continue target language learning when the rest of the class was engaged in an activity that was too simple for them, such as grammar or basic vocabulary.

Most of the students wrote about different topics each time but some chose one topic that interested them and dedicated their entire journal to it. The purpose was for every student to explore their own interests and identity. The journals were submitted to the EFL teacher once a week for feedback. The texts were not corrected in the journal. Instead, the teacher made suggestions about language use on a separate sheet of paper. The only person who wrote in their journal was the student. The comments were intended to give the students further ideas or incentives to keep writing and to provide a space for teacher-student dialogue.

A special group was created where students met in after-school hours to discuss issues of diversity, to read texts and literature dealing with diversity and to write their own creative texts. At the end of the year, texts written in the journals and texts written as part of the activities in the diversity group were published in a collective volume of student texts entitled, *We, the Others: Studying Diversity in the Social Environment of the School* (Kourtis-Kazoullis and Tzanetopoulou, 2003) (see Figure 4.6). This gave the students the incentive to write for an audience and edit their work, but also to experience actually publishing a book. All the work was done by the students themselves – the typing of the texts, editing, translating, designing the layout, etc.

Εμείς οι άλλοι:

Μελετώντας την ετερότητα
στο κοινωνικό περιβάλλον του σχολείου

Επιμέλεια:
Βασιλεία Κούρτη-Καζούλλη
Αρετή Τζαντετοπούλου

Figure 4.6: The collective volume published by the students

Outcomes

Thanks to the Identity Journals, the students' confidence to express themselves in the target language markedly improved. This seemed to be because they were given an opportunity to explore their identities and experiences in the teaching/learning process. The classroom pedagogy was also significantly different from traditional EFL instruction that seldom strayed far from the textbook. The work of two student-authors, Fotis and Besa, from the collective book *We, the Others: Studying Diversity in the Social Environment of the School* (Kourtis-Kazoullis and Tzanetopoulou 2003) depict how the Identity Journal can be used to promote transformative orientations to pedagogy.

Fotis

Fotis was was born in Saranda, Albania and he and his parents had immigrated to Greece. Two of Fotis' many texts are presented below. One is an essay in which he describes his experiences as an immigrant, and the other is a poem that powerfully portrays his feelings.

In the text '*My name is Fotis and I am from Himara (Albania)*' he introduces himself, telling us that he is 15 years old and that at home his father speaks Albanian and his mother speaks Greek or a dialect of Greek. His text is a journey into time and place where his family is forced to move from a country with political unrest and economic collapse and to wander from city to city in Greece in search of a replacement homeland. At the age of 3 his family moves to the island of Corfu and he lives there until age 6 when the family moves to Athens and he goes to school there. He describes how he begins to make friends but misses his old friends. In the middle of the 6th grade in primary school his family moves again, this time to Rhodes, where he stays for the next six years.

In class he is a cheerful and polite boy who is eager to make friends. But in Fotis' texts we establish a picture of what he has experienced and what he feels. There is no place for these feelings in the school curriculum and there is no hint of what he has experienced in the regular classroom routine.

In his poem entitled *There is only one homeland*, his classmates who read it can experience with him what immigrants or refugees may feel when forced to leave their homeland. *There is only one homeland* was published in Greek in the book *We, the Others: Studying Diversity in the Social Environment of the School* (Kourtis-Kazoullis and Tzanetopoulou, 2003) and was translated into English for this book.

There is only one homeland by Fotis
In war and in misery
And in extreme poverty,
I left my home
To open a new door, a door
That for me was, unknown
What lies behind it.
My precious homeland,
In this world I will find no other
Home like you,

So beloved and beautiful.

You will be for me, my Ithaca
And I your Odysseus.
No matter what they promise me,
No matter what they tell me,
I will have you in my heart
As a symbol so that they can see.
If they want to, they can understand.
This will be my destination,
To find you again,
Even if it means losing my sight.
A homeland equal to you and identical
many have tried to find.
But I am certain of one thing only:
'They will never find it!'
And repentant, like the prodigal son,
back they will return.

And the homeland like the Father
Will open his arms again
To embrace his children
Which will have repented.
And the fatted lamb
He will slaughter for his children,
His precious children, his greatly embittered children.

Fotis begins his poem with, '*In war and in misery and in extreme poverty, I left my home*'. *War, misery* and *poverty* are three concepts that are incomprehensible to someone who has not experienced them, but emotionally powerful for those who have. He describes his homeland as Ithaca and compares himself to Odysseus as he travels from place to place. The epic of the *Odyssey* describes Odysseus' travails as he spends ten years trying to return home after the ten-year Trojan War. Similarly, Fotis' epic poem describes his own travails as he follows his family from place to place.

He ends his poem with the parable of the Prodigal Son. He relates the life and hardships of an immigrant to the second son who becomes an indentured servant, with a degrading job. Just as the second son's father treats him, upon his return, with a generosity far more than he has a right to expect, Fotis envisions such a return to his homeland.

Besa

Besa is 19 years old. She was born in Kruje, Albania. Her mother is of Greek origin and her father is Albanian. She came to Greece when she was 15. Her mother tongue is Albanian and her second language Greek. She also speaks some Italian, as Kruje is near the coast of Albania across from Italy, and some English which she has learned at school. Her proficiency in Greek is below the level of the class so she has difficulty taking past in the lessons. She rarely speaks in class and is very quiet and hesitant to disclose much about her identity and experiences.

Two texts are presented below: one self-descriptive short text in English and one poem about a tragedy at sea near her hometown. She chooses to write the self-descriptive text in English, a neutral language, not Greek or Albanian. She writes the poem in Albanian but chooses to translate it into Greek for the collective volume *We, the Others: Studying Diversity in the Social Environment of the School.*

I left Albania when I was fourteen by Besa

I left Albania when I was fourteen years old, and I came to Greece in 1998. Now I live in Greece on an island called Rhodes. I went to high school when I came to Greece. It was difficult for me to communicate with people but after I went to school I started to speak Greek well. I met new friends, but I never forgot my old friends in Albania. I remember when I was in Albania with my friends in our classroom. When we finished the lesson the first thing we did was to meet and go to the park to play different games. I will never forget those days.

Otranto by Besa S.

Besa writes a poem entitled Otranto, referring to the 'Otranto tragedy' in March 1997 in the Strait of Otranto, a passage between southeast Italy and western Albania connecting the Adriatic with the Ionian Sea. An Albanian ship, Kater I Rades, with 105 people on board who were trying to flee the social turmoil in Albania was intercepted by an Italian navy vessel seeking suspected illegal migrants. The two ships collided and the Albanian ship sank, killing 83 people – men, women, children and babies (Gibney and Skogly 2010:72). Besa's poem speaks of people drowning and crying out for help. Her home town, Kruje, is around 20 miles from Otranto. The tragedy happened when she was 9 years old and living in Albania. She chose never to explain why she wrote the poem or whether she had family or friends on the ship.

Otranto by Besa
May that black day never come again,
When mothers raised
Their hands towards the sea
To grasp a pain that aches.

Souls scream from Otranto
Help! Help!........
It is not the call of the birds,
That fly over the waves.
It is the voices of people
Coming from black Otranto.

Impact

After the book was published, the students themselves held two seminars: one for the students and teachers in their schools and one for all the teachers in their city. The students read their texts and presented their work. They felt very proud of their accomplishments and of the fact that they were now accepted by the other students in the school. At the beginning of the school year students had been reluctant to disclose their ethnic background and identities if these differed from those of the majority of students, but by the end of the year they were more conscious of and positive about diversity. Through examining their own identities and experiences and comparing them with those of others they could see that everyone is similar but different – that diversity is a part of everyone's identity. The Identity Journal provided the environment for expression of identity and the publication of the collective volume *We, the Others: Studying Diversity in the Social Environment of the School* gave the student-authors the chance to share their identity texts with the school community and feel proud of their own identities. At the end of the year, one student used a questionnaire to conduct a study to determine how students in the school viewed diversity after reading the book and attending the seminar. The question about how students in the school viewed diversity after they had read the book and taken part in the seminar elicited interesting comments. One captures the essence of identity text work particularly vividly:

> *The diversity of each person is a treasure that lies deep within the soul. The only thing we have to do is to discover it.*

References

Gibney, M. and Skogly, S. (2010) *Universal Human Rights and Extraterritorial Obligations.* Philadelphia: University of Pennsylvania Press.

Kourtis-Kazoullis, V and Tzanetopoulou, A (2003) *We, the Others: studying diversity in the social environment of the school.* Rhodes, Greece: University of the Aegean [in Greek].

Skourtou, E Kourtis-Kazoullis, V and Cummins, J (2006) Designing virtual learning environments for academic language development. In J Weiss, J Nolan, J Hunsinger and P Trifonas (eds) *The International Handbook of Virtual Learning Environments.* Dordrecht: Springer.

Case Study 7
Multi-Language Identity Texts + Internet Technology: A Case Study in Guza, China
Jonathan Lambert

Introduction

Teachers, students and community in Guza use a variety of creative methods in language learning and teaching. For example, the Tibetan Department of Sichuan University for Nationalities (SUN) recently held an evening poetry reading contest where students and teachers shared powerful performances in Amdo and Kham dialects. Around the same time, students and teachers in the English Department organised a spectacular drama exhibition mixing Sichuanese, Mandarin and English. We are also experimenting with projects in writing and English language learning.

Among the various approaches are the ideas that a learner's first language and culture is a resource (Canagarajah, 2006), and that 'bilingual instructional strategies can usefully complement monolingual strategies to promote more cognitively engaged learning' (Cummins, 2005). Combining Internet technology and language learning, while not a panacea, can help 'the student who is trying to master a new language reach the appropriate level of academic proficiency' (Kourtis-Kazoullis Papantonakis, Makrogianni, and Kladogenis, 2009). Amidst major challenges in education and the drastic inequalities in the distribution of power in the world, combining multi-language identity texts and the Internet has the potential to create positive sites where students participate in learning, teaching and expression.

Context

Guza is located in mountains near Kangding, Dartsendo town. In surrounding areas there are rich landscapes of multiliteracies and thick layers of discourse. This case study looked at six online multi-language identity texts. They were all written at SUN from January 2010 to November 2010. They include original writing, translations and audio recordings. The writers are from a variety of ethnicities including Tibetan, Han Chinese, Yi and Kejia communities. Each writer is fluent in several languages and dialects. Participants in the study included local students, students at other universities in China, the local community and local teachers and SUN administrators. Data was collected by means of semi-structured interviews and document analysis.

Process

The multi-language stories in this case study are identity texts in the way the writers invest aspects of their complex personalities in their creative work. Each story relates to personal experience or concepts of home. The students were not instructed to write specifically on the identity text theme. It just happens to be one of the similarities among the multi-language stories.

The texts were created in extracurricular classes and were the product of mixed-methods and varied interactions. Tsewong Lhamo Wang Chunying recorded audio and wrote translations for the first of the multi-language materials in this case study, *Sacred Mountains*, after looking at *Amazing Tibetan Folktales*, a book of oral histories produced in 2008 by Tibetan high school students from Yushu. This book has a trilingual introduction. Later, as students read or heard about the *Sacred Mountains* story, several of the other texts in this case study were created.

While editing their own work, the students improved their proficiency with English language skills and produced creative, engaging compositions. Sometimes the rewriting process took weeks. Students were free to continue the editing and writing or discontinue, as they chose. Thumbnail sketches of some of the stories are presented in Figure 4.7 (from http://www. grandala. org/multilangidentitytextsgz/english.html)

Output

The most recent identity text in this case study was prepared by Droka Lhamo in November, 2010. In the middle of the editing process, she was taking additional extracurricular language classes with a former classmate from middle school. When the classmate saw her story, she glanced at the page and said, 'I want to do this too.'

> The other day, when my friend and I were walking and talking together, I saw two people. One was an old man and the other was a small boy. They walked forward hand in hand.

Figure 4.7: Selections of multi-language identity texts from Guza

> What surprised me the most was the young boy. He walked so calmly, as if he were a grownup. His small, soft hand was in his grandfather's big hand. If the boy jumped here and there like other children, his grandfather might fall down. Also, in front of where the old man was walking, it was not flat. He would pull the small hand more firmly for fear the small boy might fall down.
>
> What a wonderful sight! It seems to me that the whole world is in their hands.
>
> In their daily life, they are walking hand in hand to a bright future.

Droka Lhamo was active in the Tibetan poetry contest mentioned at the start of this chapter. Wearing traditional clothing from her hometown, she stood alone on the stage and shared a poem about a famous Tibetan teacher.

Impact

Students from a variety of places are sharing encouraging feedback about the stories and the exciting use of multi-languages together in one space. Several other students at SUN say they are inspired by the poems they have read to

ལག་རྗུང་དམ་དུ་སྦྲེལ་བ། HAND IN HAND

by Droka Lhamo རྫོ་དགའ་ལྷ་མོ།

ཉིན་ཞིག་ང་དང་གྲོགས་མོ་འཇེད་གཉིས་སྟོ་འཆམ་དུ་འགྲོ་སྐབས་
ལམ་བར་དུ་ལོ་ན་བགྲེས་པའི་རྒན་པོ་ཞིག་དང་ཕྲིས་པ་གཉིས་
ཕན་ཚུན་ལག་རྗུང་དམ་དུ་སྦྲེལ་བའི་རོ་མཚར་གྱི་དང་ཆུལ་དེ་
སྐད་ཅིག་ཉིད་དུ་ང་རང་གི་མིག་ལམ་དུ་འཆར་སྣབས། ང་ལ་
འདི་སྣ་བུའི་བསམ་རྒྱལ་ལམ་འཆར་སྲུང་ཞིག་བྱུང་། གལ་ཏེ་
ཕྱོང་གཉིས་ཀྱུག་ཀྱོག་གི་ལམ་ཕྲན་ཞིག་ཏུ་ལག་རྗུང་དམ་དུ་
མ་སྦྲེལ་བ་ཡིན་ན་ཡུན་རིང་མ་འགོར་བར་ཕྱོང་གཉིས་སར་
འགྱེལ་འགྲོ་བ་ནི་ང་ཚོས་སྟོས་མ་དགོས། ཡིན་ཏེ་ཕྱོང་གཉིས་
ཅིའི་ཕྱིར་མཉམ་གཉིས་བྱེད་པ་ཡིན། ཅིའི་ཕྱིར་ལག་རྗུང་
དམ་དུ་སྦྲེལ་བ་རེད། གྲོགས་པོ་ཆོ་སྦྱིར་བཏང་དུ་གོ་ལ་རྒྱམ་
པོ་འདིའི་སྟེང་འཆོ་བཞིས་ཏུ་བཞིན་པའི་མི་གང་ཞིག་ཡིན་རུང་
ཕན་ཚུན་གཅིག་ལ་གཅིག་བརྟེན་གྱི་འབྲེལ་བ་ཆགས་ཡོད་པ་
ནི་ང་ཚོས་མིག་མཐོང་ལག་ཟིན་རེད། དེ་བས། ང་ཚོས་ཕྱིམ་
གཉིས་ཆེན་པོ་འདིར་འབྱུང་འགྱུར་གྱི་ཡོད་རེར་སྐྱོང་ཕྱུན་
གྱི་བགྲོད་ལམ་ཞིག་འཆོལ་དགོས་ན་ཕྲོག་མར་ལག་རྗུང་
དམ་དུ་སྦྲེལ་དགོས་པ་ནི་ངྡོན་འགྲོའི་ཆ་རྐྱེན་ཡིན་ལ། ང་བརྗོད་
ང་ཚོའི་མ་འོངས་པའི་འཆོ་བ་དེ་ལའང་དོན་སྐྱིད་ལྔན་སྲིད་དོ།

produce their own creative writing. The website currently presenting the six identity texts in this case study will continue to grow.

The stories discussed in the present case study received positive response from teachers:

> *... impressed and delighted... wonderful gifts for storytelling and desire to use language. With this practice, students at all levels can quickly learn how to engage in other activities to further their skills.* (Liu Chengping, Dean of the English Department at SUN)

> *While reading the stories, I think it's a new way to learn language. I think it will be very helpful for those who are learning different languages. I hope the work can continue to get better.* (Bema Tserang, teacher at SUN)

> *... very good, especially the layout of the Tibetan language is really good. Then I add some other English and Tibetan on the site where learners can learn a lot.* (Riyak, a teacher in Yushu and student in Xi'an)

The writers of the six multi-language texts offer further insights into this kind of identity text project. As Droka Lhamo wrote in a recent email:

> *I read my story. I think it is good. I'm also reading a story written by my best friend, Yixi Zema. I am so happy.*

References

Canagarajah, A S (2006) Toward a writing pedagogy of shuttling between languages: Learning from multilingual writers. *College English* 68(6) <www.outreach.psu.edu/programs/rsa/files/toward_a_writing_pedagogy_of_multilingual_writing.pdf>.

Cummins, J (2005) Teaching for cross-language transfer in dual language education: Possibilities and pitfalls. Paper presented at the TESOL Symposium on Dual Language Education: Teaching and Learning Two Languages in the EFL Setting, Bogazici University Istanbul, Turkey <www.achievementseminars.com/seminar_series_2005_2006/readings/tesol.turkey.pdf>

Kourtis-Kazoullis,,V Papantonakis, G. Makrogianni, T and Kladogenis, D-I (2009) An Internet-based learning environment for the teaching of Greek as a second language through literary texts: Theory and practice. In Close, E Couvalis, G, Frazis, G, Malaktsoglou, M, and Tsianikas M (eds.) Greek Research in Australia: Proceedings of the Biennial International Conference of Greek Studies, Flinders University June 2007. (321-334). Flinders University Department of Languages – Modern Greek: Adelaide. <http://dspace.flinders.edu.au:8080/dspace/bitstream/2328/8085/1/321-334_Kourtis-Kazoullis%20et%20al.pdf>.

Case Study 8
'I Am Becoming More Intelligent Every Day': 'Non-native' English student teachers' liberating Identity Texts

Mario E. López-Gopar

Mexico's geographical proximity to the USA seems odd when one thinks of the wide gap between Mexican English teachers and the so-called native speakers of English. The native speaker spectre still haunts Mexicans (see Clemente and Higgins, 2008, and Clemente *et al* this volume). The consumers of the English language seek gringo-looking English teachers – fair-skinned and blonde – in the belief that they are more competent than Mexican English teachers. Hence, Mexican English teachers – typically perceived as brown-skinned – struggle between hanging on to their roots or turning into the elusive native speaker (López-Gopar, Stakhnevich, León García, and Morales Santiago, 2006).

Like many 'non-native' English teachers around the world, Mexican English teachers ignore or forget that they are bilingual or multilingual and possess multi-competences (Cook, 1999). In order to counteract the ideological colonisation of the English language (Pennycook, 2007), language teacher educators must engage in critical dialogue with future English teachers so as to reinvent new identities in which their local knowledge can be reconstructed and revalidated. The creation of identity, texts works as a catalyst for this critical dialogue. In addition, as Kamler (2001) argues, 'it is through the processes of designing [stories/identity texts] that writers produce new representations of reality and at the same time remake themselves – that is, reconstruct and renegotiate their identities' (p54).

Context

In 1992, Mexico signed – or, as many believe, were forced to sign – the North American Free Trade Agreement (NAFTA). One of the effects of NAFTA was an exponential growth in the demand for the English language, even though many Mexicans still held ambivalent feelings toward the USA and the English language. English teacher preparation programs also began to emerge. The case study presented here took place in the first of such programs, established in 1991, in the state of Oaxaca. Oaxaca is the most culturally and linguistically diverse state in Mexico, with sixteen Indigenous languages officially recognised as national languages (INALI, 2008). Following up a three-year ethnographic study (Clemente and Higgins 2008) and a call for critical pedagogies in the teaching of English in Mexico (Clemente *et al*, 2006), my student teachers and I began contesting the imposed and derogatory discourse that positioned us as incompetent 'non-native' teachers of English. We did so through the creation of bilingual and/or multilingual identity texts during the 'Teaching English to Children' (TEC) course I taught in the BA program in English teaching at the public state University of Oaxaca.

Process

In the TEC course, we used identity texts as mediational tools to negotiate our identities. Ada and Campoy (2004) stress that teachers need to create their own identity texts if they want to connect with their students and create an inclusive and welcoming classroom environment where the teacher-student divide is overcome. Identity texts can also be viewed as mirrors in which students' and teachers' identities as intelligent, multilingual, talented individuals are reflected back to them (see Chapter 1).

During the TEC course with the student teachers, I created my own identity text in order to achieve three objectives: to share with my students my own sense of who I am and my own constructed identities; to connect with them at a more personal level; and to provide a model for the identity texts they were to create. (For samples of my identity text, see López-Gopar, 2009.) Since I am a competent multilingual person, my identity text was written in Spanish, English and French. It used a range of modalities, such as photos, video, and sound.

For their identity texts, some student teachers created traditional paper-based books, others created posters, and others PowerPoint presentations. Each created two identity texts: one about themselves and the other about someone important in their lives. While doing this, the student teachers shared their texts with each other and kept a diary about their reflections on the course readings and their connections to the Oaxacan context. The identity texts included Spanish, Italian, French, English, Japanese, and five different Indigenous languages from Oaxaca: Chatino plus four varieties of Zapotec. Some student teachers shared their identity texts with the whole class, while others shared with small groups. All were surprised at one another's fascinating lives, creativity, and multi-competences.

A student-author identity text

In the following narrative, I present the first part of one of the identity texts created by Luis, a student teacher in the TEC Course, and try to recreate Luis' presentation of his identity text to the class. (For other student teachers' identity texts, see López-Gopar, 2009.) Luis was the most courageous student in class – he decided to go first and share his bilingual (Spanish/English) identity text, a PowerPoint presentation entitled, 'The Many Things I Am.'

Luis begins:

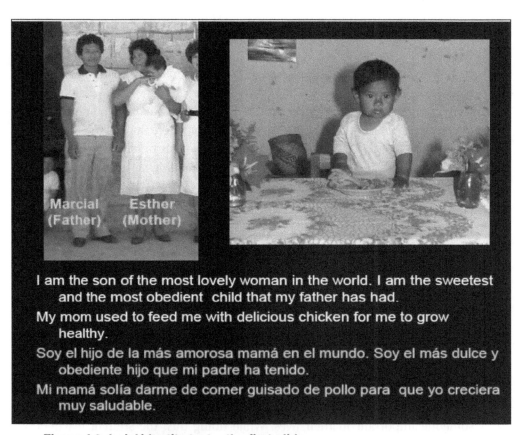

Figure 4.8: Luis' identity text – the first slide

The class responds with 'ahhs', giggles, and looks of approval. Proud of his humble origins, Luis continues with the next slide, in which he portrays himself at age 8 with his two younger siblings and tells us his nicknames: 'I am called 'Drian' at home, 'Cueto' at school, and 'Tutillo' by all my five uncles at work.' Luis' family is very important to him, especially his grandmother: 'I am the child number two in my family and the first grand-son that my granny had, too.' With his identity text and the consent of his classmates, Luis not only performs his bilingual competence but also solidifies his awareness that he is a very intelligent person: 'I am a very hardworking boy. I was the strongest and smartest kid in kindergarten. In fact, I am becoming more intelligent every day.'

Impact

Luis' confidence in his talents and awareness of his growing intelligence has had a ripple effect on himself, his classmates, and on me as his teacher educator. We all started to realise that pejorative identities, such as being labelled as a deficient 'non-native' speaker, can and should be contested by re-examining our identities. During the TEC course, the student teachers and I learned that if we want to change the grand narratives, such as the supremacy of the native speaker that places us in the category of deficit, we need to start telling our own stories *back* as a way of resistance. It is only through this dialectical relationship between grand narratives and personal stories that change and liberation are possible (Kamler, 2001). In order to exorcise the (English) native speaker (Clemente and Higgins, 2008), our identity texts shifted from 'standard English' to multilingual narratives. Our voices told stories about how important our parents are, how intelligent we are, how much our family and friends care about us, how much we enjoy the little things in life, and how committed and caring we are as educators, among much else. We hope that our identity texts will encourage other non-native teachers from around the world to explore the multi-competences, intelligence and creativity they possess.

References

Ada, AF and Campoy, I (2004) *Authors in the Classroom: a transformative education process*. New York: Pearson/Allyn and Bacon

Clemente, A Crawford, T Garcia, L Higgins, M Kissinger, D Lengeling, MM Lopez Gopar, M Narvaez, O Sayer, P Sughrua, W (2006) A call for a critical perspective on English teaching in Mexico. *MEXTESOL Journal Special Issue: Critical Pedagogies*, 30(2), p13-17

Clemente, A and Higgins, M (2008) *Performing English with a postcolonial accent: ethnographic narratives from Mexico*. London: Tufnell Press

Cook, V (1999) Going beyond the native speaker in language teaching. *TESOL Quarterly*, 33, p185-209

INALI (2008) *Catálogos de lenguas indígenas nacionales*. Retrieved September 8, 2008, from http://www.inali.gob.mx/catalogo2007/

Kamler, B. (2001) *Relocating the Personal: a critical writing pedagogy.* New York: State University of New York Press

López-Gopar, ME (2009) 'What makes children different is what makes them better': Teaching Mexican children 'English' to foster multilingual, multiliteracies, and intercultural practices. Unpublished Doctoral Dissertation, University of Toronto, Toronto, Canada

López -Gopar, ME Clemente, A and Sughrua, W (in press). Co-creating identities through identity texts and dialogical ethnography. *Writing and Pedagogy*

López -Gopar, ME Stakhnevich, J León García, H and Morales Santiago, A (2006). Teacher educators and pre-service English teachers creating and sharing power through critical dialogue in a multilingual setting. *MEXTESOL Journal Special Issue: Critical Pedagogies*, 30(2), p83-104

Pennycook, A (2007) ELT and colonialism. In J Cummins and C Davison (eds.) *International Handbook of English Language Teaching* (Volume 1). New York: Springer

Case Study 9
Getting students to document linguistic diversity

Dolors Masats
Virginia Unamuno

Introduction

Due to migration movements, Catalonia, an autonomous region within the Spanish state, has experienced rapid population growth in the last decade. In such a context, it seemed relevant to investigate and document the emerging multilingual practices of both the local population and the new citizens. Accordingly, our project aimed to explore the continuities and discontinuities between school and non-school communicative practices by describing and analysing the processes of language socialisation undertaken by two groups of secondary students. It was our view that by taking into account students' particular interpretation of the socially accepted procedures of language use (Unamuno, 2009) in their various communities of practice, and by tracing the emergence of new linguistic repertoires and new identities (Codó and Patiño, 2010), we could shed new light on how language education might be carried out in a multilingual milieu such as ours.

Context

Our research was conducted in the reception classrooms of two high schools, one in the city of Barcelona and the other in a neighbouring town. Reception classrooms have a mediating role for newcomers or students with special educational needs, as they are intended to help their integration into mainstream classrooms. So it is not surprising that most of the students in our study were of immigrant origin (30 out of 48).

We wanted to capture the essence of how social actors categorise languages, describe language practices and construct their identities. Accordingly, data was gathered by the students themselves, who made a short documentary film on their multilingual practices in their school and neighbourhood. The observation of the process of video production, together with the analysis of the different outcomes, allowed us to describe how students in the study redefined their 'linguistic repertoires' (Blommaert, Collins and Slembrouck, 2005), and affiliated with existing or emerging groups.

Process

The project was conducted during the academic year 2008-2009. Teachers in both schools allowed us to implement a language project to get their students to document multilingual practices in and outside the school, on condition that the project contents included some elements of secondary education curriculum, which were decided on collaboratively with the teachers. Although the groups in the two schools were not from the same grade level, we were able to negotiate a focus on the same four topics in the schools. The students in each group were divided again into four smaller groups, each of which was responsible for documenting one of the topics in the project. The topics were specified in the school curriculum in the area of language:

- Multilingualism
- Linguistic varieties (of Catalan and Spanish)
- Visual communication
- Non-verbal communication

Outcomes

During the process of producing documentaries, students undertook tasks which led them to challenge traditional conceptualisations of identity investment. We briefly cite three:

- **Catalan identity as a monolithic construct** – In the documentaries, students interviewed some of their teachers who were Catalan speakers. During the interviews, the topic of language variety was put forward and students invited their interviewees to narrate situations in which they had felt 'discriminated against' or 'uneasy' because they spoke a variety of Catalan other than the official one (the one they have to teach at school). These communicative episodes can be regarded as identity texts, in the sense that they allowed participants to question the validity of 'Catalan identity' as being a monolithic construct.

■ **Identity as a trait of origin** – During the process of writing the scripts for the videos, students explored the idea of identity as a socially constructed trait linked to conflicting processes of membership categorisation. Thus, they defined the 'Latin identity' as a personal trait bound to certain musical and clothing preferences, to the use of a new emerging variety of Spanish and to ways of behaving and interacting. To the students who identified themselves as 'Latin', their identities were not linked to their countries of origin because not all the young people born in South America were viewed by them as Latin, whereas certain local students (from Catalonia) were accepted as Latin. Their membership categorisation conflicted with that of their teachers, who associated the Latin identity with all – and only – those students born in Central or South America.

■ **Identity as a group trait** – In this case, the identity text is to be found not in the discourse generated during the process of creating the videos, but in one of the video documentaries. In the video, students took medium close-up and extreme close-up shots of people's shoes and trousers, as a way of illustrating that identity is closely linked to certain clothing styles. What was interesting here was not only the process of deciding what would be included in the video, but especially the fact that while making the video recording, they learned that the choices made were not that obvious for their audience. This led students to see that identity traits such as outward appearance are not always mutually recognisable across groups.

Impact

The project served to document the existence of two voices in the school – the institutional voice, which is expressed through Catalan, and the voices of the school community which are expressed through a variety of languages in all forms of communication: oral, visual and written. The project implementation helped both students and their teachers to become aware that although language practices in and outside the school are not always the same, language diversity is a shared trait in all the communities of practice they belong to and should therefore be a focus of inquiry in the school as a means to guarantee social inclusion.

References

Blommaert, J, Collins, J and Slembrouck, S (2005) Spaces of multilingualism. *Language and Communication*, 25(3) p197-216

Codó, E and Patiño, A (2010) Language choice, agency and belonging at a multilingual school in Catalonia. Paper presented at Sociolinguistics Symposium 18, University of Southampton, UK

Unamuno, V (2009) Dinàmiques sociolingüístiques i immigració: l'escola com a microcomunitat. In C. Junyent *et al* (ed). Llengua i acollida. Barcelona: Horsori

Further reading

Corona, V Tusón, A and Unamuno, V (2008) Falar el nosotros de allá y el de ellos de aquí: a variacion do castelán como obxecto de reflexion e de ensino. In MT Diaz García, I Mas Alvarez and L Zas Varela (eds). *Integración Lingüística e Inmigración.* Santiago: Lalia-Universidade de Santiago de Compostela

Websites

The videos produced by the students can be viewed at http://linguamonaudiovisual.cat

Search codes: PVMulti; EDOMulti; PVCNV; EDOCNV; EDOVA; PVCG; EDOCG; PVVA

The webquest used to develop the video making project is available at: http://greip.uab.cat/es

Case Study 10
The Multimodal Discursive Construction of a Dancer on YouTube as Identity Text
Kim Meredith

Introduction

This case study can be seen as a response to Pennycook's (2010) recent call for educators to 'grasp the different digital worlds of identification that our students inhabit as well as [the] interplay between the flow, fixidity and fluidity of culture, language and identity'. Ten years ago, Lam (2000) developed the notion of 'textual identity' to understand how English language learners composed texts to represent and reposition their identities in computer-mediated environments. In the decade since her study, the community of practice of the Internet has shifted. The growing popularity of YouTube in particular has opened up new multimodal design possibilities for the construction of identity and entry into new communities of inter-mediated practice. This case study seeks to explore this digital world and its affordances for identity text production and dissemination.

Context

The data for this study comes from the YouTube channel of YouTube user 'GallantxD2,' henceforth referred to as 'Gallant.'[1] In his YouTube profile, GallantxD2 chooses to list his occupation as 'A.R. MacNeill student.' Further, he identifies his hobbies as 'Guitar, Singing, Dancing, and Building anything,'[2] and books as 'I hate books and the library, you say library, i scream' (GallantxD2, YouTube profile). Through these discursive choices, Gallant constructs his textual identity in line with many discursive practices (music, videos, dancing, singing, playing the guitar), but in opposition to print literacy practices. Although Gallant's first language is Tagalog, all his YouTube communication is in English. With the exception of two videos[3], all of his 19 videos

111

currently uploaded relate to dance.[4] The video entitled 'Gr. 8 Portfolio 2008-2009' (available at http://www.youtube.com/user/GallantxD2#p/a/u/2/E5Q Wgq3MCSg) has been selected because it intertextually combines many of the other videos on the channel and is simultaneously a school assignment and part of his constructed online world.

Process

The title of this video labels it as a 'grade 8 portfolio.' As explained on the school's website, all students in the school 'are required to complete a portfolio presentation of their learning at the end of the year' (A.R. MacNeill website, http://www2.sd38.bc.ca/MacNeill-Web/Portfolios). The standard portfolio assignment sheet (available at the same website) lists the content and criteria required for portfolio completion: 'One example from each academic and elective area class'. A project that exceeds expectations 'presents portfolio in original/imaginative way' and 'organises student's reflection of learning and clearly shows personal growth'. The portfolios are presented to and evaluated by a teacher, a parent and a peer. By not specifying the modality and by encouraging connections across the curriculum and to lives and audiences beyond the classroom in both time and space, the portfolio becomes a potentially rich identity text. This student in particular demonstrates his identity investment by posting the project on his YouTube channel.

Output

The text Gallant has produced is a remarkably multimodal identity text that constructs his identity as simultaneously a successful student and an active member of the online dance community. The initial title slide greets his audience with words and the sounds of J. Han and Sam Ock's popular hip hop anthem *Never Change* and states the designer's intention (reprinted here with original spelling and grammar): 'Heyo/this video, focuses, on comparing dance, to what ive learned throughout the year/Comparing subject like,/ science, math and French/To tutting, waving and contemporary (respectively)' (0:00-1:13, *sic*). What follows is an eight-minute video intertextually combining ten videos of himself dancing various styles, four videos of famous dance crews (winners of America's Best Dance Crew) competing, two videos of his high school seniors performing, seven images of the school dance team, seven audio tracks (in addition to the songs already in the videos), and 46 titles or captions in six different fonts. He layers a written simile over a video of himself and a friend performing his first piece of choreography to compare dance to art because 'choreographing a dance, is like painting a picture, where every move is a stroke of the brush' (0:41); he layers words over a video of himself attempting a contemporary piece to compare contemporary dance to French because 'French is a different language for most of us/ You could say that about contemporary, for us hip hop dancers/See I never was good at French OR contemporary ANOTHER similarity =]' (5:06-5:56). Finally, he compares dance to the 'eras and communities' he learned about in humanities by referring to the 'eras' of dance and defining dance as 'a community on it's own' which he describes in yearbook-like fashion, showing images of the dance team with phrases such as 'We learn from each other' superimposed and DRU's sentimental hip hop anthem Seasons playing in the background (6:56-8:26).

Impact

A Bakhtinian analysis (Bakhtin, 1986) of the intertextuality and addressivity of this multimodal text reveals that many of the author's generic, style and compositional choices can be seen as constructing the utterance for the sake of the teacher's positive evaluative response. In fact, the video is described on YouTube with the descriptor 'I GOT A FREAKING A! =D' and the comment that the grade he got 'exceeds expectations in all categories,' thus recognising that he did successfully construct this complex utterance to meet the generic expectations of the institutional portfolio assignment. Where this text differs from many school assignments, however, is that it shows signs of being at least equally[5] designed for a secondary, authentic[5] audience beyond the walls of the classroom. As an intertextual examination shows, this utterance has been constructed in such a way as to be positioned also in the sphere of the YouTube dance community, where he receives positive feedback in the form of views (378 as of May 10, 2010), ratings (currently rated 4 out of 5 stars), and comments.

Comments for this video demonstrate how identity texts can reflect back an identity in a positive light in which students receive 'positive feedback and affirmation of self in interaction with ... audiences' (Cummins et al, 2006:6). Responses include the simple but significant 'aha nice nice =]' from a senior dance team member and general praise for the idea behind the utterance, including 'OOOO and this was An AMAZING idea haha. I might do something like this haha lol.'

This indicates the way that this utterance has the potential to affect the field of the online dance community, the school dance community, and the school classroom community. By bringing them together in new ways, the possibilities for meaning-making are multiplied. The Redesigned is presented as an Available Design (New London Group, 2000) for other members to use in their meaning-making endeavours, especially bringing dance into the scholastic realm.

Notes

1 A pseudonym for the purposes of this study.

2 He also lists movies as 'i like movies, all i can say :],' music as 'Anything i can dance to, VICTOR KIM :D,'

3 One of a spider eating a smaller spider and another of an 'Asian Hair Tutorial for Curly Hair'

4 Five are videos he has recorded and uploaded of other dancers performing/competing at school or district dance events and the remaining 12 are of himself dancing. Two of these 12 are of him dancing with others (as part of a Global Fusion school dance group and as part of a duo at a school talent show) while the rest are solo dance videos. The solo dance videos include several sub-genres: c-walking videos, help-request videos, freestyle dedication videos, and two school projects involving dance. One of these school projects is a project for humanities while the other is entitled 'Gr. 8 Portfolio 2008-2009.'

5 I use Purcell-Gates' (2008) definition of 'authentic' as 'real-life' literacy practice rather than 'school-only.'

References

Bakhtin, MM (1986) *Speech genres & other late essays.* Austin: University of Texas Press

Cummins, J Bismilla, V, Chow, P. Cohen, S, Giampapa, F, Leoni, L, Sandhu, P, Sastri, P (2006) ELL Students Speak for Themselves: Identity Texts and Literacy Engagement in Multilingual Classrooms. Retrieved from http://www.curriculum.org/secretariat/files/ELLidentityTexts.pdf

Dru (2008) 'Seasons' [song]. On *The One* [album].

GallantxD2 (June 15, 2009) *Gr. 8 Portfolio, 2008-2009* [video]. Retrieved November 18, 2009, from http://www.youtube.com/user/GallantxD2#p/a/DA77D5061842CF0A/0/E5QWgq3MCSg

Lam, SE (2000) L2 Literacy and design of the self: A case study of a teenager's writing on the internet. *TESOL Quarterly* 40 p.183-203

New London Group (2000). A pedagogy of Multiliteracies designing social futures. In B. Cope and M. Kalantzis (eds) *Multiliteracies: Literacy learning and design of social futures.* London: Routledge

Ock, S and Han, J (April 6, 2009) *Never Change* [song and video]. Retrieved December 11, 2009, from http://www.youtube.com/watch?v=462GNf0nl4c

Pennycook, A (2010). Nationalism, identity, and popular culture. In N. Hornberger and S. McKay (eds). *Sociolinguistics and language education,* Bristol: Multilingual Matters.

Purcell-Gates, V (2008) Real-life Literacy Instruction, K-3: Handbook for Teachers. The Cultural Practice of Literacy Study, UBC. Available at http://www.authenticliteracyinstruction.com/

Further reading/viewing

http://www.youtube.com/user/GallantxD2#p/a/u/2/E5QWgq3MCSg

Case Study 11
Identity Affirmation through Story Writing
Rania Mirza

Introduction

With the rapidly changing cultural demographics of schools, administrators and teachers are increasingly challenged to meet the needs of their diverse student populations. In Ontario, a range of policy and support documents have been published in recent years to support teachers in addressing the learning needs of diverse students (http://www.edu.gov.on.ca/eng/teachers/publications.html). Administrators and teachers use the term 'multicultural education' frequently, but what does this mean? What is multicultural education? What does it look like in the school system? These are questions that I've reflected upon deeply.

In my view, education is about building relationships between administrators, teachers, students and the community, encouraging the student voice in the classroom, and affirming student identity through the careful selection and creation of classroom resources and units. It is about teaching students that their ideas and experiences count inside and outside the classroom.

This case examines how I used the genre of story writing to actively engage my grade 7 and 8 English language learners (ELLs) in a process of creating identity texts, thereby enabling them to see themselves in the curriculum. The unit objectives included learning how to organise thoughts, develop characters, settings and plot lines, and write descriptively with an audience in mind. The broader goals of the unit were to help my students see themselves as writers and to acknowledge that their voices and ideas were important.

Context

I am a teacher in the York Region District School Board in Ontario, Canada. The K-grade 8 school I teach in has a diverse student body of about 700 students. Last year, I had the opportunity to be the ESL teacher for grades 3-8. Going into this classroom assignment, I already knew or had heard about many of the students who would be in my ESL class. These were students who were often either silent in mainstream classrooms or who defiantly acted out. But why? I was determined to use my classroom to find out.

I taught my grade 7 and 8 students in a withdrawal setting for a few language periods a week. Even though most of the students had moved to Canada from their native homelands around four years earlier, many were still at early stages of English acquisition.

Process

I began our narrative unit by sharing a story with the class that was told to me by my parents when I was young, a story rich with content from my Islamic heritage. I then invited my students to orally share stories that they were familiar with. They were able to recount familiar Western fairytales such as Cinderella, but when I probed them for stories that were personal and unique to their own cultures, they were silent. An Afghani boy finally mumbled that he couldn't really remember any Afghani tales and that they weren't any good anyways. I didn't want to push, so I began reading them narratives from various cultural backgrounds, carefully selecting texts that were representative of my students' heritage. I wanted them to see themselves, their parents and their communities in the resources we shared. Instantly, the students were able to connect the tales to their own lives or to stories from their own cultural identities. This led to a deeper, more personal and invested analysis of all of the texts.

I told the students that they would have the opportunity to write their own stories. Not many were excited about the idea, as they saw it as merely an assignment. I began conducting individual conferences with the students to help them brainstorm ideas. I initiated the conversation by suggesting that they could use events from their own lives or from the lives of people they knew. This was problematic as the children didn't believe they had ever experienced or witnessed anything worth writing about. During our discussions, I engaged them in exploratory questions that focused on their backgrounds. The students began to engage eagerly, because they recognised the relevance to their lives.

My class recognised that I was truly interested in their stories and this amazed them. After overhearing a conference I had with one of his peers, Sajad, a grade 8 learner, commented, 'Miss, you're so interested! How come you're so interested? Now that I know that, I have a story to tell you too!' The ideas started to flow. Some of the students had the same L1, so I encouraged them to share ideas with each other in their native tongue. For them this was a unique experience in a classroom setting – teachers had always told them they were only allowed to speak English in school. Soon the classroom was buzzing with stories that took place in Uzbekistan, Afghanistan, India and Turkey. There was a new energy in the room.

Output

The identity text I've chosen to highlight is a story written by a 14 year-old Afghani boy, Sajad, and translated into Russian by his classmate, Arina. The story was also translated into Farsi, Sajad's home language, with the help of an educational assistant at the school. Sajad wrote a story about a neighbourhood soccer match in Uzbekistan. Sajad is the protagonist in the story and he names his other characters after his cousins and friends in Uzbekistan. The story is filled with action and drama, as the captains of the opposing teams are sent to jail for fighting over the soccer match. The story ends with the team captains apologising to each other and becoming friends.

Sajad's story served as a bridge to welcome Arina into our class when she arrived at the school in mid-year. She had been living in Canada for just over a year, after moving from her homeland, Russia. She was a shy, reserved, beginner English language learner who had literacy skills in Russian. Arina made an instant connection with Sajad, because he had grown up in Uzbekistan, a country that she was familiar with, and he knew some basic Russian.

While the rest of my students were busy completing their final version of their stories, I decided that I wanted Arina to take part in the activity too. So I encouraged her to work with her knowledge of Russian and quickly partnered Arina with Sajad. Her task was to translate his story, 'Narrative Fights for Soccer' into Russian. She enjoyed following Sajad's comical plot-line and Sajad was proud that he was able to help her learn some English. When the task proved to be too challenging for Sajad, I enlisted the assistance of one of my colleagues, who was fluent in Russian, to aid in the translation process. Arina took the story home to get her older sister to help her with the English translation. She was dedicated to this writing task and was happy that by the end, she too had a story to share.

Impact

In the course of this unit, all the students were able to create stories they were proud of. They saw themselves as authors. When describing the writing process Sajad commented: 'When I'm writing about my own ideas, it's easy to write'. One of the final stages before publishing was for the students to write an author's note and Sajad decided to describe the beauty of Uzbekistan in his note. A student who had once been reluctant to share anything about his cultural background, now felt it necessary for his readers to know more about his country.

The enthusiasm evoked by this narrative writing unit carried on throughout the year. The students saw themselves as competent readers, inquisitive investigative reporters, opinionated debaters, passionate actors and, of course, comedians. Empowered and engaged, active, alive, previously silent – and silenced – young students, were now freely sharing, exploring and open to receiving. And for me, a truly profound experience.

Further reading/viewing
Sajad's trilingual story (English, Farsi, Russian) can be viewed at http://www.oise.utoronto.ca/lar.

Case Study 12
Identity Texts in a Sister-Class Context: How are ELL students' voices heard?
Jacqueline Ng

Introduction

Research has reported that global learning networks have the potential to promote L2 learning both in and out of school by providing students with ample opportunities for authentic L2 use (eg Man and Lim, 2003). This case study was intended to explore how ELL learners can benefit from the creation of identity texts through a sister-class network that enabled them to collaborate with geographically distant partners in carrying out projects that were connected to the language arts curriculum but entailed active literacy engagement in researching and writing about topics of mutual relevance and interest.

Context

Two grade 7 classes from Canada and Hong Kong communicated through a project website set up specifically to facilitate the cultural and academic exchange. All the participating students were learners of English, who tend to be stereotyped and positioned in relation to their still developing English language and literacy skills. The students from the Canadian school were new immigrants who had been living in Canada for less than five years. Some had difficulty expressing themselves orally or producing grammatically correct writing. The students from Hong Kong were learning English as their second language and as a mandatory subject in an EMI (English as the medium of instruction) secondary school.

A significant number of secondary students in Hong Kong experience ongoing difficulties in learning curricular content through English. This challenge is even greater for students who are transferred from CMI (Chinese as the medium of instruction) primary schools to EMI secondary schools. The sister-class project sought to offer language teachers in both the Canadian and Hong Kong contexts ways to help students improve their literacy skills and succeed academically, by negotiating their identities in a student-centered pedagogical space. Data collection for the study included class observational reports, interview transcription analysis, participants' online discussions, and their project presentations.

Process

The participating students co-created a cultural artifact with their sister-class partners by selecting a topic that matched their own interests with the curriculum goals, researching relevant materials from a variety of sources, exchanging information, sharing opinions, and constructing an identity text together in the online learning context. The topics they chose covered a wide range of interests including festivals and food, travel, nature and environment, sports, and pop culture. The students all had basic computer literacy skills to communicate with their partners and work together on the project website. Partly because of the technological learning environment, the students were highly motivated to learn how to post online messages, texts and images for peer review and feedback, as well as how to design and create innovative PowerPoint slides to make their own identity texts. They were also given a choice to generate a bilingual product by translating the identity texts into their L1 with the help of their parents. At the end of the unit, students presented their cultural artefacts to their teachers, principals, parents, and students from other classes. The identity texts were published on the project website to celebrate students' academic accomplishments and to further affirm their identities through the positive feedback they received from active interaction with their audience.

Output

The study provides evidence for the claim that online collaboration in the co-construction of knowledge represents a powerful and dynamic force for learning by virtue of the fact that it activates students' previous experience and builds on and extends their existing conceptual and technological skills. One of the sister-class groups, which worked on the topic *Travelling around the World*, developed a creative, well-presented identity text that described the most famous attractions of Canada and Hong Kong (see Appendix 1). A

Canadian student and a Hong Kong student from this group wrote a brief introduction, derived from information they had researched on the Internet that discussed the population, climate, history, and geographical features of their home countries. Some of the new concepts posted by the Hong Kong student on the discussion forum were difficult for their partners and class-mates to understand, for example, 'special administrative region' (SAR), 'Basic Law', 'legal and social system'. The teachers took advantage of this teachable moment and asked the students to look up the meaning of these terms from a dictionary or other online sources and write down the meaning, with illustrative examples, on handouts prepared by the teacher. By sharing appropriate findings from the Internet, the students effectively learned the colonial history of Hong Kong through an engaging discussion of related terms such as 'the British Empire', 'the First Opium War', 'military defence', 'China regained sovereignty', 'autonomy' and so on (see Appendix 2).

The students created an attractive layout of the travel booklet on the computer and were extremely proud to showcase the cultural heritage and beauty of their respective countries. They were also excited to share their own stories of visiting these attractions, and to incorporate some appealing pictures taken either from the Internet or their own trips. This group produced the identity text in two languages, English and Chinese, to show appreciation for their own cultures and re-affirm their personal linguistic and cultural identities.

Impact

Interviews with students and teachers suggested that literacy engagement derived from the opportunity and experience to actually become authors, take ownership of their intellectual and creative work, and to share this work with family and friends outside the school context. One student expressed these feelings like this:

> I've never [thought] that I could do a project with my classmates on the Internet. It is amazing that we could find information and images from [different] web-sites and then chat with my group on the computer. The slides we made on PowerPoint are cool and I can't wait to send our booklet to my friends and family. I like this project very much!

A Canadian teacher confirmed these sentiments, speaking about the reaction of her students:

> My students greatly enjoyed working online with their peers because they could exchange ideas in a very interesting and casual way. They were excited to get to know and collaborate with students from a foreign country to produce an

academic project together. They were motivated to create their text through PowerPoint constituted by their own knowledge and experience, first language input, imagination, and artistic talent. They were very proud to show their project to their parents, overseas families and friends, and other students in the school.

Reference

Man, E. and Lim, J. (2003) Promoting use of the Internet in English language teaching. *Journal of Basic Education*, 12(2), p156-174.

Appendix 1: Students' identity text: 'Travelling around the world'

Canada and Hong Kong

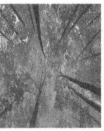

Canada

In the world the second largest country is Canada. Canada has 9.9millon sq.km. The major city is Toronto ,Montreal and Vancouver. Canada's climate varies. At Places it is cold all year long but in Toronto is it cold in the winter and really hot in the summer.

Hong Kong

150years ago Hong Kong has described as a "barren rock". HK is a world-class financial , prading and business centre. HK only has a natural resources it was finest deepwater ports .

After1.7.1997 HK been a special administrative region (SAR)of the Peole's Republic of China . Under the Basic Law, HK will be maintained for 50 years in legal and social system .

Man-made Attractions in Canada

Canada has many attractions. Those attractions made by humans could be divided into three groups: amusement parks, malls and monuments.

There are many theme parks in Canada. For example, Paramount Canada's Wonderland which is Canada's first theme park is one of the best amusement parks in the world. There are over 200 exciting attractions and over 60 thrilling rides. In this theme park, there is also a 20 acre water park. Paramount Canada's Wonderland is north of Toronto off Highway 400 and just ten minutes north of Highway 401.

In the Niagara Falls region, there is a very unique theme park called Marine land. This is a very special attraction since it is not only a theme park but also a place where you can meet many animals such as deer, bears, killer whales and many, many more. Marine Land is at 7657 Portage Road which is one mile from Horseshoe Falls.

The last amusement park that I will include is CNE. This is an annual fair held near the heart of downtown Toronto. It was founded in 1879 and there are 65 rides along with a large food court and many shows. Here, they have an annual celebration of Chinese New Year. At this celebration, you can see lion dances, martial arts and many other Chinese traditions. You can also buy many things that are related to the Chinese culture.

123

加拿大和香港

加拿大

加拿大是世界上第二大国家，有990万平方公里。主要城市有多伦多，满地可和温哥华。加拿大的气候各地都不相同，有些地方终年寒冷，而多伦多则冬天寒冷，夏天炎热。

香港

150年前香港还只是一个贫瘠的渔村，而今天的香港则是国际级的金融贸易中心。香港是一个天然的深水良港。自1997年7月1日起，香港成为中华人民共和国的一个特别行政区，按照基本法，香港将维持法律和社会制度50年不变

加拿大人建造的景点

加拿大有许多景点。我想人造的景点主要分为三大类：包括游乐场，商场和纪念碑。

加拿大有许多主题公园，加拿大的第一个主题公园是Paramount Canada's Wonderland。园内有二百多个景点和六十多个机动游戏。园内还有一个20英亩的水上乐园。Wonderland在多伦多以北400高速公路的旁边，只是401高速公路以北十分钟的车程。在你家拉瀑布附近有一个非常独特的主题公园叫Marineland。说它特别是因为它不仅是一个主题公园，而且在那里你能见到各种各样的动物像鹿，熊和杀人鲸之类。Marineland的地址是7657Portage Road离开瀑布大约一英里远。我在这里要讲的最后一个游乐场是CNE，这是在多伦多市区中心每年举行的一个节日。首届节日在1879年举办。园内有65个机动游戏和很大的美食广场和许多表演。

加拿大有许多商场，但我将只介绍其中一个，那是West Edmonton Mall，它是世界上最大的娱乐和购物中心，也是阿伯特省的第一景点，场内有超过800家商场和110家食肆，商场面积相当于48个街区。

加拿大也有许多的纪念碑，The Lefebvre历史遗址是为了展现Acadians在1755年被驱逐出境后的生活写照。此遗址坐落在New Brunswick东南部的Memramcook Valley内，另一个加拿大著名的纪念碑是Brock's纪念碑。此纪念碑是为了纪念Brock将军在1812年为抵御美国军队的进攻在指挥Queenston高地防御战中捐躯而建。纪念碑在1840年4月17日被炸，现在看到的185英尺高的纪念碑是1859年重建的。

Appendix 2: Students' discovery of online resources

Hi guys,

I found the meaning of SAR and the Basic Law of Hong Kong from this website: http://en.wikipedia.org/wiki/Hong_Kong

Can we use it in our project?

Hong Kong (<u>Chinese</u>: __) is one of two <u>special administrative regions (SARs)</u> of the <u>People's Republic of China</u> (PRC), the other being <u>Macau</u>. Situated on China's south coast and enclosed by the <u>Pearl River Delta</u> and <u>South China Sea</u>, it is renowned for its expansive skyline and deep natural harbour. With a land mass of 1,104 km² (426 sq mi) and a population of seven million people, Hong Kong is one of the most <u>densely populated areas</u> in the world. Hong Kong's population is 95 percent ethnic <u>Chinese</u> and 5 percent from other groups. Hong Kong's <u>Han Chinese</u> majority originate mainly from the cities of <u>Guangzhou</u> and <u>Taishan</u> in the neighbouring Guangdong province.

Hong Kong became a colony of the <u>British Empire</u> after the <u>First Opium War</u> (1839-42). Originally confined to <u>Hong Kong Island</u>, the colony's boundaries were extended in stages to the <u>Kowloon Peninsula</u> and the <u>New Territories</u> by 1898. It was <u>occupied by Japan</u> during the Pacific War, after which the British resumed control until 1997, when <u>China regained sovereignty</u>. Hong Kong's <u>independent judiciary</u> functions under the <u>common law</u> framework. Its political system is governed by the <u>Basic Law of Hong Kong</u>, its constitutional document, which stipulates that Hong Kong shall have a 'high degree of autonomy' in all matters except foreign relations and military defence.

Anything else you have found? Please share more!

Case Study 13
Drama as Identity Texts in Ugandan HIV/AIDS Clubs

Bonny Norton

Introduction

Uganda has drawn on diverse and innovative practices to educate the population, including school children, about the origin, spread, and effects of HIV/AIDS. Mushengyezi (2003), for example, has conducted research on rethinking indigenous media as forms of public communication in Uganda, arguing that drama, storytelling, and 'talking drums' have been effective in conveying messages on poverty eradication, HIV/AIDS awareness, and immunisation in rural communities. Stein's (2008) research in South Africa also has relevance for understanding the power of drama in disseminating information about HIV/AIDS. Drawing on her research with young African students, Stein explores adolescent sexuality through students' visual texts, which, she argues, allows them to draw the 'unsayable' (p.75). In a world in which adolescent sexuality is culturally marked by silence, she makes the case that a range of semiotic modes can be used to express fear, violation, pain and loss.

Context

In 1997, Uganda began a skills-based education program for HIV/AIDS prevention, developing school health policies on HIV/AIDS, school-based counselling, and HIV/AIDS school clubs (UNAIDS, 2004). In a 2003 study with grade 11 students from four different schools in eastern Uganda, HIV/AIDS clubs were identified as a major source of information on the epidemic (Mutonyi, 2005). The case study presented here draws on a follow-up study, conducted in 2004, which examined to what extent HIV/AIDS clubs drew on multiliteracy and multimodal resources to share information on HIV/AIDS

(Norton and Mutonyi, 2007). The participants in the study were student club leaders, teachers and health officials. Data collection included question-naires, interviews, document analysis, and observation of club activities.

Process

In our follow-up study, we found that most of the dramatic performances included mimes, poetry, songs, skits and role-plays interspersed with short messages. The performances were conducted in English, the official language in Uganda, although it is a second language for this multilingual population in which over 60 languages are spoken. The performances can be defined as 'identity texts' in that they engaged not only the cognitive abilities of stu-dents, but also their identity investment. As I have noted in prior research (Norton, 2000:10-11; and in press), the construct of 'investment' conceives of the language user as having a complex identity, changing across time and space, and reproduced in social interaction. All the performers in the HIV/AIDS clubs were highly invested in their dramatic productions, partly because they were able to take on multiple identities and to perform what is often unsayable in many communities in Uganda.

The dramatic performances also involved writing, as the student members of the HIV/AIDS clubs edited, practised and polished their scripts for the pur-poses of presentation. A student leader noted that all performances conveyed messages in a 'simplified language, which in most cases contain the students' private dialect' (Norton and Mutonyi, 2007:485). The use of a 'private dialect' is best understood as an attempt to take ownership of English, and create investment on the part of the audience as they observed and interacted with the performers. Importantly, audience participation was an integral part of meaning-making in the dramatic performances of the HIV/AIDS clubs. Members of the audience were not passive observers, but helped to co-con-struct the meaning of the identity texts through vibrant interjections, choral participation, enthusiastic clapping, and ongoing commentary.

Output

The particular identity text chosen for this case study is a dramatic poem pre-pared by a young woman, Penina Nafuye, which was performed at an AIDS club meeting in a rural Ugandan school on a Sunday in 2004. I was present at the meeting, and observed how charged the atmosphere was, and how ener-getically the audience participated in the dramatic performance, particularly with respect to the choral sections of the following text:

CHOICES FOR YOUNG PEOPLE

When preparing for a dance there are two choices

You either go for the dance or you don't go for the dance.

If you don't go for the dance, that's fine.

But if you go for the dance, my friend, there are two choices

You either dance or you don't dance

If you don't dance, that's fine

But if you dance, my friend, there are two choices

You have to either dance with a partner or you dance alone

If you dance alone that's fine.

But if you dance with a partner, my friend, there are two choices

You either dance close to her or far away from her

If you dance far away from her, that's fine.

But if you dance close to her, my friend, there are two choices

You either go home with her after the dance or you leave her there

If you leave her there, that's fine.

But if you go home with her, my friend, there are two choices.

You either sleep with her or you don't sleep with her.

If you don't sleep with her, that's fine.

But if you sleep with her, my friend there are two choices.

You either have sex with her or you don't have sex with her

If you don't have sex with her, that's fine.

But if you have sex with her, my friend, there are two choices

You either have protected sex or unprotected sex.

If you have protected sex, that's fine.

But if you have unprotected sex, my friend, there are two choices.

You either get the virus or you don't get it

If you don't get it, that's fine

But if you get it my friend there is one choice, That's death.

Thank you very much. It is so sad.

Impact

The impact of using drama to educate young people about HIV/AIDS is profound. The words of the club chairperson in one school, as noted below, were echoed by many students and teachers in Uganda (Norton and Mutonyi, 2007:485):

You see, students will usually not turn up in big numbers when you are giving a talk on HIV/AIDS. So we thought that maybe if we organise the drama as a sort of entertainment for the school, we could have many students attending and we can use the opportunity to talk about HIV/AIDS. The drama is always about HIV/AIDS, but it is also fun so students come to watch and listen. Drama is a very good way of communicating HIV/AIDS to the students.

Penina's poem, in particular, has had an international impact because I video-taped it with a digital camera, and made it available on YouTube, my website and on publicly available plenary addresses such as the 2009 IATEFL conference (see websites below). The meaning of the poem that is co-constructed with each viewer and audience is a function of the investment of both performer and viewer, in the context of the multiple and changing identities of all the participants in the dramatic event.

References

Mushengyezi, A (2003) Rethinking indigenous media: Rituals, 'talking' drums and orality as forms of public communication in Uganda. *Journal of African Cultural Studies* 16, p107-128.

Mutonyi, H (2005) The influence of pre-conceptual and perceptual understandings of HIV/AIDS: A case study of selected Ugandan biology classrooms. MA thesis, University of British Columbia.

Norton, B (2000) *Identity and Language Learning: gender, ethnicity and educational change.* Harlow, England: Longman/Pearson Education.

Norton, B (in press) Investment. Routledge Encyclopedia of Second Language Acquisition. London and New York: Routledge

Norton, B and Mutonyi, H (2007) Talk what others think you can't talk: HIV/AIDS clubs as peer education in Ugandan schools. *Compare: Journal of Comparative Education*, 37(4), p479-92.

Stein, P (2008) *Multimodal Pedagogies in Diverse Classrooms: representation, rights and resources.* London and New York: Routledge.

United Nations AIDS (UNAIDS, 2004). Life-skills-based HIV/AIDS education in schools. Available on line at: http://www.unaids.org/ungass/en/global/UNGASS19_en.htm (accessed November 11, 2004).

Further reading

Higgins, C and Norton, B (eds) (2010) *Applied linguistics and HIV/AIDS.* Bristol, UK: Multilingual Matters.

Kendrick, M, Jones, S Mutonyi, H and Norton, B (2006) Multimodality and English education in Ugandan schools. *English Studies in Africa*, 49(1), p95-114.

Websites

YouTube: http://www.youtube.com/watch?v=jzV6nHN03yY

Bonny Norton website: http://www.lerc.educ.ubc.ca/fac/norton/

British Council Cardiff Online: http://iatefl.britishcouncil.org/2009/sessions/63/plenary-session-bonny-norton

Case Study 14
Multilingualism as an Academic Resource
Diane Potts

In linguistically diverse communities, there is always a danger of isolating the language of education, the language in which science and technology, law and government are carried on, from the languages of daily life (Halliday, 1986/ 2007:304)

The crux of the matter is that we need to think of issues such as linguistic in-equality as being organised around concrete resources, not around languages in general but specific register, varieties, genre ... the challenge is to think of language as a mobile complex of concrete resources. (Blommaert, 2010:47)

Introduction

It is all very well to discuss multilingualism as a substantive resource for meaning-making, but quite another to imagine highly diverse classrooms in which students regularly and consciously choose to draw upon their multi-lingual resources in the production of everyday academic texts. Blommaert's words help us identify the challenge before us more clearly. It is not – or not only – associated with the diversity of languages in our classroom, not only with the things we label English, Bengali, Xhosa or Portuguese. Rather, the challenge is more productively framed around our students' concrete lin-guistic resources, and the question we as educators might ask ourselves is how we can support students in drawing upon the specific registers and genres of their everyday lives – the concrete resources they regularly and creatively employ outside of school – to further their academic success.

For students whose home and school registers and genres closely align, the usefulness of such resources may be relatively transparent. For students whose resources are characterised by dissimilarities and disjunctures, redres-sing inequality requires a more strategic effort on our part. Quite frequently, our pedagogies must not only scaffold the design skills needed to put such resources to use, but also support students in reassessing the value of their resources. This vignette sketches one attempt to do exactly that.

Context

Within the context of The Multiliteracy Project, MJ Moran's grade 6-7 classroom was one of the more active Vancouver research sites. The students' texts authored during this and a second research grant exemplify the richness of the classroom practices, and the texts produced by these ethnically and linguistically diverse students reflect knowledge that students brought to school, as well as classroom learning. (Note that the teacher, MJ Moran, does not use the term 'identity' to describe the work of her students, nor to conceptualise her teaching practice). However, despite encouragement and exhortation, the students' use of their home languages was limited and superficial. Their lives but not the languages of their lives were employed in their academic work.

In the year following The Multiliteracy Project, MJ's students voted to complete a unit that would force them to use their home languages. Some of the students had been part of the earlier academic study, some had not. The students chose to take on this extra unit of study knowing that they would be using their languages in ways that had not been observed in the previous research study. The output of that unit can be viewed at http://multiliteracies.ca/index.php/folio/viewGallerySlideShow/250/545.

More than anything else, the extra unit provided clear evidence of just how strongly the students had classified their home languages as neither appropriate nor valuable to their academic studies. The extent to which these attitudes disadvantaged some children was glaringly apparent to everyone. This second point was most startling to multilingual students whose home language was not English, and who were succeeding academically. As one student reflected:

> We noticed that people had acted differently when they were speaking their first languages. A student, Mia, came from China. She doesn't speak English well, yet. She was confident in speaking her first language in front of everyone. We found this interesting, because she is usually quiet and during these classes she always participated ... John is uncomfortable to speak in front of the class in English. He does not often offer answers or lead conversations. Using our first language (Cantonese), he was one of the students that always participated.

Following the unit, students appeared to accord home languages greater status, and the students' classroom interaction suggested they were more comfortable bringing their languages into the classroom. But this did not necessarily translate into understanding of the strategic meaning-making potential of their home languages. Consequently, in the following year (now two years after the completion of the initial research), we thought further about what needed to happen in the classroom. MJ described the lessons' genesis in her accounts of her pedagogic practices:

> Diane and I had previously discussed how the students naturally represented their understandings using modalities when preparing projects, and that possibly with direct instruction and opportunity to develop this natural tendency their projects might extend themselves even further.

Process

Three lessons on multimodal design, each $1^1/_2$ hours long, were inserted into the regular cycle of the study of a novel, *Zack* by William Bell. The three lessons were thematically organised around the title 'Everything Means,' and introduced students to the concepts of mode (The New London Group, 2000), of design and visual grammar (Kress and van Leeuwen, 1996/2006), and of interactivity (Goodman, 2006). Drawing on these resources, students analysed visuals, museum exhibits and other forms of text and assessed the contributions of each mode to the text's meaning.

Within the context of these lessons, students viewed several items from an exhibit at the Museum of London. In this exhibit, immigrants had written postcards in their home language describing the experience of immigration. The postcards were written in a range of languages and translated into English, and a community member had responded to the card. The students were shown the home language and translated versions of the postcards as a means of bringing languages into the discussion of multimodality.

One of these cards was written in Spanish. Their classmates were intrigued when the two Spanish-speaking students, one whose place of origin was the Dominican Republic and the other's Guatemala, read the original Spanish aloud and discussed the differences in their pronunciations. When asked if their understanding of the Spanish and English texts differed, the two initially said no. However, when probed with more specific questions, the young woman described the differences in her feelings when reading the two texts. Her description was effective but not always coherent; she said how hard she found it and to describe the differences in her feelings across the two languages. That struggle also intrigued her classmates, and was a point of empathy among her multilingual classmates. So although the translations opened the door for discussion, it was the students' observations of their peers' efforts that led to greater self-reflection. The challenges of meaning-making across languages and the impact of the students' languages on their understandings of the world had been made visible.

Output

The students' novel projects, reflections on their novel projects, and assessment of the lessons on multimodality are open to the public, and can be viewed at http://multiliteracies.ca/index.php/folio/viewProject/249. Because the interest of this vignette is specifically on students' use of their multilingual resources, we look more closely at Kristine's project. Kristine was in grade 7 at the time, and was one of two Tagalog speakers in the class. Her novel project combines linguistic, visual and spatial elements to create an interactive text (see http://multiliteracies.ca/index.php/folio/viewDocu ment/249/11541). Kristine describes her project as follows:

> After planning and studying the book more i finally found the project I was going to do. I did something called a 'Zack Box' It was mainly focusing on *feelings*. The 'Zack Box' included a box with main images from each chapter, and quotes in English and Tagalog. I let the people who were looking at my project include themselves in it rather than just looking at it. They either had to choose an image and write down what part it was in the book just by looking at it, pick a quote and say which language gave more meaning, and or pick a part in the book that made them feel a feeling.

The book was of course written in English. The Tagalog quotations were Kristine's translations of key moments in each chapter, translations she undertook to further explore her emotional response to the novel.

Impact

In MJ's class, students regularly reflect on their projects and on their learning. In reflecting on her novel project, Kristine writes 'People seemed interested in my project so it made me happy ...This is one of the best projects I made...I learned different modes and media and information I need to make a project that had meaning.' MJ concurs. Kristine's project displays greater depth of comprehension and analytical sophistication than she had ever before achieved in Language Arts.

The texts, not the students, are the research subjects for the study, and so it is not possible to describe the milestone this text represents in Kristine's academic development. It is possible, however, to state unequivocally that the milestone was marked by an expansion in Kristine's understanding of herself as resourced, by an increase in her multimodal design skills, and by a shift in her capacity to adopt a metalinguistic (or, more appropriately, metasemiotic) perspective on her academic activities. These achievements are Kristine's; the practices which supported her achievement were built up across several years, as the students in this combined classroom increasingly came to see their multilingualism as a resource for their academic learning.

References

Blommaert, J (2010) *The Sociolinguistics of Globalization*. New York: Cambridge University Press

Goodman, S (2006) Literature and technology. In S Goodman and K O'Halloran (eds) T*he Art of English: literary creativity.* New York: Palgrave MacMillan

Halliday, MAK (1986/2007) Language across culture. In JJ Webster (ed) *Language and Education, Volume 9 in the Collected Works of M.A.K.* Halliday. New York: Continuum

Kress, G and van Leeuwen, T (2006) *Reading Images: the grammar of visual design (2nd ed)*. New York: Routledge

New London Group (2000) A pedagogy of Multiliteracies: Designing social futures. In B. Cope and M. Kalantzis (eds) *Multiliteracies: literacy learning and the design of social futures.* New York: Routledge

Case Study 15
Let Me (Re)tell You My Story:
Creating trilingual identity texts at an
orphanage school in Burkina Faso
Gail Prasad

Introduction

Multilingualism is the norm in West African countries. Although Burkina Faso's official language is French, it has fourteen recognised indigenous languages as national languages, and 59 different languages are spoken there (Lavoie, 2008a). Formal schooling has traditionally been conducted only in French, as it was during its colonial past. In 1996, however, the government of Burkina Faso passed a law to allow the use of national languages other than French in school. Although the process of parental petitioning for a local school to adopt a bilingual model is not without its challenges, Lavoie (2008a, 2008b) describes the benefits of bilingual education in Burkina Faso and the capacity of bilingual teaching to support students' multilingual and multiliteracies development. At a time when Burkina Faso's education system was transitioning towards bilingual education, this research project sought to examine how bilingual teaching strategies could effectively be integrated in classroom practice. How could a multilingual approach to literacy development support linguistically diverse students' engagement at school?

Context

The case study describes fieldwork conducted in 2008 at an orphanage school located 40 kilometres outside Ougadougou, the capital city of Burkina Faso. The elementary school was established to serve orphaned children aged 6-12 from over ten villages. This aim of this research was to assess language and literacy practices of teachers and students at *l'École Nouveau Départ*

135

(pseudonym) and to support teachers in constructing a bridge from students' diverse oral language and cultural practices to print-based literacy development at school. Data collection included classroom observation, teacher and administrator interviews, document analysis and a number of classroom activities with students including the creation of linguistic self-portraits, inspired by the work of Busch, Jardine and Tjoutuku (2006), and students' drawings of literacy practices (Kendrick and Jones, 2008; Kendrick and McKay, 2004).

Process

After conducting teacher interviews and class observation, I worked primarily with one teacher to facilitate the creation of three trilingual multimodal books by students aged 9-12. This bookmaking project was conceptualised within a multiliteracies framework (Cope and Kalantis, 2000; Omoniyi, 2003). The goal was that the published books would become part of the library that was being established at the orphanage. It was hoped that these identity texts would showcase students' plurilingual abilities, allow teachers and students to see their diverse linguistic resources and cultural practices affirmed as tools for learning within the classroom, and encourage students to take ownership of the library.

After introducing me to his students, the classroom teacher asked them to work in groups to brainstorm traditional Burkinabé tales that are shared in the home villages through oral storytelling. With an assortment of French picture books I brought along for this project, I then had students analyse how print and images work together on the pages of a book to tell a story. Next, as an example of the multilingual books we would create, we read *Un Inukshuk Solitaire* (1999), a bilingual French-Inuktitut book written by fifteen grades 5-7 students from Nunavut, Canada. Together, we discussed how French (one of Canada's official languages) and Inuktitut (an official language for the Inuit people in Nunavut) were used to recount the importance of the Inukshuk in Arctic life for the Inuit. From this story, students recognised how recording their traditional Burkinabé tales in Mooré and French and illustrating them would allow them to preserve and retell their stories from their own perspective.

Students worked in groups to retell their versions of a traditional tale and then to create a composite version that could be translated into French. The text was written in French first because students had not formally learned to write in Mooré at school. Students who were fluent in Mooré worked with their teacher to translate the French text back into a written Mooré. I translated the

French text into English so that the story would be more widely accessible and because these students would be learning English when they graduated from elementary school. Once the written versions of the text in French, Mooré and English had been edited, other students worked on illustrations for each section. The text was formatted using Microsoft PowerPoint on a Macintosh laptop. A different colour and font were used to distinguish each language. Photos were taken of each of the illustrations that had been created using oil pastels and drawing cardstock. The text and images were put together to create an electronic book.

Students were able to read their trilingual e-books on the laptop. We recorded the teacher and students reading the story aloud in French for the first time, as well as their oral retelling and singing of the story in Mooré. When I returned to Canada, I exported the slides that had been created in PowerPoint as images to iPhoto – a photo editing program available for the Macintosh. I could then create a photobook within the application and I had it printed by mac.com. Hard copies of the books were sent back to *l'École Nouveau Départ* for their school library.

Output

The focus of this case study is the trilingual (re)telling of '*Kiibg Naongo – La soufrance d'un orphélin – An Orphan's Plight.*' A sample page (Figure 4.9) illustrates how typography was used to differentiate among the three languages, and also how pastel images were reproduced through photography throughout the book. An electronic version of the book can be viewed at: http://web.me.com/gprasad/eportfolio/Research.html

Impact

'An Orphan's Plight' was the first trilingual book completed during this research project in 2008. The story recounts the tragedy of Nani when she is orphaned by her mother's death. The children at *l'École Nouveau Départ* are all attending the school because they too have been orphaned by the death of their mother, father or in some cases both. Admittedly, I was at first concerned about the brutality recounted in the story. In keeping with the desire to encourage students to tell their own stories and to develop their own voices, I held back from expressing my concerns until they finished the story. While the moral at the end of the story warns against violence, the ultimate benefit of listening to their entire story was that they felt their experiences affirmed within the pedagogical space of the classroom.

*Il était une fois, un homme vivait avec ses
deux femmes: Tené et Tella. Il aimait
beaucoup Tella, la plus jeune, et détestait
Tené la première. Tené et Tella avaient
chacune une fille: Nani et Nina. Mais Tené
possédait des richesses et elle achetait
beaucoup de vêtements pour sa fille, Nani.*

Rao n da tara a pagba yiibu: a Tené ne a Tella a
ra nonga a pugbilfa Tella la a kisga pug kudra a
Tené ne tella ra tara ned faa bipugla ye: a Nani
ne a Nina. la a Tené paonga ra yiida a Tella la a
ra raada Teed wusgo in konta biiga Nani.

Once upon a time, there was a man who had two wives
named Tené and Tella. He loved Tella, the younger one, very
much but he didn't like Tené, his first wife. Tené and Tella
each had a daughter: Nani and Nana. But only Tené was
rich enough to buy everything she wanted, including lots of
clothes for her daughter, Nani.

Figure 4.9: Facing pages from An Orphan's Tale

As students re-told stories that are a part of their oral culture and literacy practices in Mooré, they recognised that they had many stories that they could write, illustrate and share with others. When they were able to see themselves as authors and co-constructors of meaning through the creation of this trilingual identity text, they were inspired to continue writing in both French and Mooré. After seeing the students' creative multilingual texts, the school administrator decided to continue bilingual writing by setting up a school newspaper. Although he had been reluctant to integrate bilingual teaching strategies at the outset of this project, he recognised through this experience how teachers and students could use Mooré effectively as a bridge to working in French. Seeing bilingual teaching in reality at his school inspired further creative practice. The classroom teacher was also able to capitalise on writing in French and Mooré to build students' metalinguistic awareness by having them compare writing conventions in both languages. Students were proud not only of the books they created through this project but also, more profoundly, of themselves as authors, illustrators and individuals with meaningful experiences and stories to share with one another and with the world. The impact of this project has indeed reached beyond the orphanage and school as the trilingual book, 'An Orphan's Plight' has been shared internationally through the partnering Canadian NGO and various research presentations.

References

Busch, B Jardine, A and Tjoutuku, A (2006) *Language biographies for multilingual learning* (Vol. 24). Cape Town: PRAESA Occasional Papers

Cope, B and Kalantzis, M (eds) (2000) *Multiliteracies: literacy learning and the design of social futures*. New York: Routledge

École Inuglak. (1999) *Un Inukshuk solitaire*. Markham, ON: Festival du Livre

Kendrick, M and Jones, S (2008) Girls' visual representations of literacy in a rural Ugandan community. *Canadian Journal of Education*, 31(2), p371-404

Kendrick, M and McKay, R (2004) Drawings as an alternative way of understanding young children's constructions of literacy. *Journal of Early Childhood Literacy*, 4, p109-128

Lavoie, C (2008a) 'Hey, Teacher, Speak Black Please': The educational effectiveness of bilingual education in Burkina Faso. *The International Journal of Bilingual Education and Bilingualism* 12(1), p1-17

Lavoie, C (2008b) Developing multiliteracies through bilingual education in Burkina Faso. *Educational Research and Review*, 3(11), p344-350

Omoniyi, T (2003) Local Policies and Global Forces: multiliteracy and Africa's Indigenous languages. *Language Policy*, 2, p133-152

Case Study 16
Quilting Our Communities:
Creating personal and collective
identity texts through the integration
of the Arts in a Grade 3 class
Gail Prasad and Nancy Dykstra

Introduction

The arts can play a powerful role in expressing diverse cultural and personal identities. Although at times the Arts risk being neglected in academic programs, a significant body of literature continues to advocate the value of integrating the arts as a methodology for learning in schools (eg Goldberg, 2006) and more broadly for qualitative social research (eg Knowles and Cole, 2008). From an instructional perspective, hands-on experiences with the arts create occasions through which children can develop their voices in alternative media and become motivated to write with authentic purpose (Ada and Campoy, 2004). From a research perspective, the arts provide a way of accessing and understanding the voices and experiences of participants without limiting them to communicating primarily in words (eg Diaz Soto and Swadener, 2005).

Context

This case study describes a collaborative project that was part of a larger research study investigating students' mobilities – geographically, socially and virtually. The larger study was funded by a grant to Dr. Diane Farmer from the Canadian Social Sciences and Humanities Research Council (SSHRC). It seeks to understand students' experiences by using the arts to allow children and youth to share their personal stories. It was supported in part by ArtsSmarts Waterloo Region, in partnership with the local school board. The objective of the partnership is to enable teachers to work with local artists to teach non-arts subjects such as social studies, mathematics or science, through the arts. SSHRC and ArtsSmarts' support made it possible for Nancy Dykstra, a classroom teacher, and Gail Prasad, a doctoral student, to collaborate with Pat Lockyer and Judy Gascho-Jutzi, two quilters from the Waterloo Region Quilters' Guild. Together, the group designed and implemented a 6-8 week project that used the art of quilting to help teach the grade 3 social studies unit on early settlers and, at the same time, allowed students to tell stories of their personal communities.

The school is located in a suburban area of Kitchener, a mid-sized city about 100 kilometres west of Toronto. Approximately 40 different home languages are spoken by the school's population of about 700 students (Kindergarten to grade 6). The school hosts families who have immigrated from about 60 countries around the globe. In the participating grade 3 class, a number of students speak different home languages, including Korean, Turkish, Vietnamese, Arabic, Romanian, Chinese and Greek. The vast majority of these students were born in Canada.

Process

Before Pat and Judy, our professional artist quilters, joined the classroom, Nancy worked with her students to develop background knowledge about early settlers and quilting. As a class, they read stories about quilts, including *Selina and the Bearpaw Quilt* (Smucker, 1995) and *The Rag Coat* (Mills, 1991). They analysed how quilts tell stories and hold memories. In addition, students brainstormed what and who make up a community, and began to make connections to their own personal communities (social, cultural, geographic, hobbies, etc).

With her background as a visual arts consultant, Pat led students through activities that helped them learn elements of design and develop basic sewing skills. Judy brought a number of her quilts in for students to explore at first hand. She shared her expertise and passion for embellishing quilts using a variety of textures, colours and found materials.

As a whole group, we decided that the question we wanted our quilt to answer was 'What is my favourite community?' Each student chose a community that is important to them and designed a square for the quilt that would tell the story of their community. Over the course of four weeks, students worked to assemble their quilt squares, using different fabrics and a variety of embellishments. Throughout the process, they spent time thinking, talking and

Figure 4.10: Community Stories quilt

working through the stories of their quilt squares. Once students had finished their squares, they were asked to write down their community stories and their artistic choices. These written pieces became their artists' statements.

The class collectively decided how their squares would be arranged in the quilt and as students continued polishing their stories, Pat and Judy sewed the squares together. With the students' final versions of their stories, Gail created a book using a photo of each students' quilt square and his/her artist's statement. She also recorded students reading their stories in order to make a multimodal electronic book.

Output

Both the quilt and the book, *Community Stories* functioned as individual and collective identity texts for the students who created them. Each student's square reflected back an important personal community beyond the classroom of which they are a member. Students' artists' statements not only facilitated their personal storytelling but also affirmed their identities as artists. When the students saw their quilt squares sewn together, one remarked with pride, 'It looks like professionals made it!' Through the project, students came to see themselves as creative artists and co-constructors of knowledge.

The audio recording of students' artists' statements allowed them to hear their stories played back in their own words and with their own voices. The use of multiple media to share their community stories made it possible to share these identity texts in a variety of ways. The class quilt and a copy of their book were donated to the local annual Mennonite Quilt Auction to support Mennonite international relief efforts. The quilt was featured in the auction catalogue and website. The School Council mobilised and purchased the quilt and book at the auction for $600.

Prior to the auction, the quilt was displayed at the school's 10th Anniversary celebration and it was hung at the local Joseph Schneider Haus museum during Quilt Month. The quilt and book are now on display in the school office for students, teachers and community members to view.

Impact

This project was by design collaborative and through the process of working and creating together, students, teachers, artists, researchers and numerous classroom volunteers became a community. Judy and Pat regularly remarked about the enthusiastic welcome they received from the students and their feeling of mutual engagement as the project unfolded. Parents, grandparents and community members who had not been involved with the school before joined the class regularly on quilting days and became integrated as valued contributors to the class. Further, the funds raised by the quilt will be used to support children and families in other parts of the world.

The children experienced themselves as part of a larger community, an impact which aligns in a tangible way with one of the school's identified values: recognising and improving our interconnectedness with others. The students' pride, individual and collective, in their accomplishment was profound. When they received their own copies of the catalogue, one student exclaimed, 'We're famous!' quickly echoed by others. Sharing the quilt publicly at school and at the Joseph Schneider Haus museum allowed students to see their class' community reflected back in a positive light. They were proud of each other's work and how it had all come together.

Nancy observed that some students did their best writing of the year for this project. This can be attributed partly to the engagement that came from having personally meaningful content, and an authentic purpose and audience for the writing. An ESL teacher highlighted the fact that the project was ideal for English language learners because students' language development and writing were scaffolded by the time invested in brainstorming with words and images, representing through quilting, collectively learning relevant vocabulary, and talking about their ideas and stories before starting to write. Finally, in a post-project interview, one student reflected that he was thankful that the class had done this project because otherwise he wouldn't have known his story. He had chosen his family as his favourite community so he had asked his mother to tell him the story of how his family came to Canada. By designing his quilt square to tell the family's story, he learned more about himself personally and was able to share what he was learning in a creative way in the classroom and beyond.

References

Ada, AF and Campoy, FI (2004) *Authors in the Classroom*. Boston: Pearson/Allyn & Bacon

Diaz Soto, L and Swadener, BB (eds) (2005) *Power and Voice in Research with Children*. New York: Peter Lang

Goldberg, M (2006). *Integrating the Arts: an approach to teaching and learning in multicultural and multilingual settings* (3rd ed). Boston: Pearson Allyn and Bacon

Knowles, JG and Cole, AL (eds) (2008) *Handbook of the ARTS in Qualitative Research: perspectives, methodologies, examples and issues*. London: Sage

Mills, LA (1991) *The Rag Coat*. New York: Little Brown Books for Young Readers

Smucker, B (1995) *Selina and the Bearpaw Quilt*. Toronto: Lester Publishing

Further Reading

ArtsSmarts website: www.artsmarts.ca

New Hamburg Mennonite Relief Sale website: view quilt #179 www.nhmrs.com

To view the 'Community Stories' ebook and more on the project: http://web.me.com/gprasad/eportfolio/Research.html

Case Study 17
Identity Texts for Teacher Training in Multicultural Society

Jérémie Séror, Amanda Hennessey
and Nico Paluzzi

Introduction

While Canada has long taken pride in its reputation as a multilingual and multicultural country, these qualities have always been accompanied by important questions and debates. In the field of education, some of the most serious of these center on schools' ability to respond to the increasingly dominant presence of linguistically and culturally diverse students in Canadian classrooms and the consequent need to rethink traditional teaching approaches and curriculum (eg Gunderson, 2007). Concerns have also focused on the training and preparation of teachers to work effectively with multilingual students in response to disconcerting reports that pre-service teachers frequently feel unprepared and uncertain at the prospect of facing diversity in the classroom (Jacquet, 2007; Moldoveanu and Mujawamariya, 2007).

For universities and teacher education programs this has meant re-examining the practices and educational provisions of pre-service teaching programs in order to bring about a situation where teachers able to handle classrooms' multilingual and multicultural reality 'are no longer a luxury but a necessity' (Garcia *et al*, 2010:135).

Context

This case study reports on work conducted in an undergraduate course taught by the principal author to pre-service language teachers on the principles and best practices associated with the achievement of linguistically and culturally diverse students. The course, *Language education in a multi-cultural and minority setting*, explores the history, theoretical foundations and educational policies of multicultural and anti-racist education in Canada. Throughout, the main objective is to equip future teachers with the knowledge they need to make informed decisions when faced with the realities of a multicultural classroom.

Process

A key principle for the course entails getting class participants to experience for themselves the same practices and activities proposed as effective pedagogy for their future students. For instance, when discussing theories of pluri-lingualism (Moore and Gajo, 2009), students partake in language awareness activities to highlight their own multiple languages and contributions to the class' linguistic repertoire.

To illustrate the impact of identity texts and a multiliteracies approach for the education of language minority students, students are asked to produce their own multimodal identity texts as part of a semester-long group project. The assignment is explicitly presented as a chance to experience the benefits of complex, collaborative and self-selected (ie meaningful) projects. Students are also strongly encouraged to draw on, in addition to more traditional resources, alternative sources of information (eg parents, fellow students, community resources) and modes of literacy (cartoons, podcasts, photography, video, amongst others).

When students hand in their projects at the end of the semester, the results have never failed to impress me. Whether it is a multilingual activity book for students or a case study of minority parents' efforts to help their autistic child attend school, these future teachers almost invariably present their projects with pride and a deep sense of engagement.

Output

One project which clearly illustrates the potential of Identity Text projects for teacher training was produced by the co-authors of this report, Amanda Hennessey and Nico Paluzzi. For their project, Nico and Amanda chose to explore through the creation of a short documentary film what at first appeared to be a deceptively simple question: Are we multicultural? The finished work not only made it clear how complex the answer to this question was, it also brought together voices and opinions from friends, reporters, teachers, principals and even politicians, capturing with a refreshing realism and honesty the tensions that characterise the contrast between ideal definitions of multiculturalism and what actually occurs and is said 'in the real world'.

As with other projects, I was impressed not only by the quality of the finished product but also by the impact this project had on Nico and Amanda. They were the first to report the documentary had taken them far beyond their original question, changing how they saw themselves as teachers and their relationship with other key players shaping multiculturalism in today's schools. Summarising this reflection, Nico and Amanda comment in the documentary:

> Nico: I think it is really important we establish we are two students making this documentary.
>
> Amanda: Yeah, it started off as a school project where we were trying to answer the simple question: Is Canada multicultural?
>
> Nico: But we quickly realised that this question actually is not that simple to answer... It's clear there is ambiguity surrounding what the definition of multiculturalism is and what it means to Canadians and Canada.
>
> Amanda: At the street level, cultural groups are not interacting, partially because of racism but also because of linguistic discrimination and overall cultural ignorance.
>
> Nico: The government assumes teachers are teaching multiculturalism, while teachers take for granted that since the government has made official policies, students, as Canadians, are naturally multicultural.
>
> Amanda: There is a serious lack of communication about whose responsibility it is to maintain multiculturalism. Meanwhile students are graduating with misconceptions of what Canada really is.
>
> Nico: If we're going to stand by the fact that we are multicultural then we have to recognise the issues and at least talk about them. We have to take an active role in trying to fix it.
>
> Amanda: But how?

Impact

To this day, Amanda and Nico continue to try and answer this question, as the project has taken a life of its own, serving as a catalyst for reflection and debate not only for them, but also for all lucky enough to view their documentary. At each viewing, audience members have celebrated their work and the hope implied by the presence of future teachers able and willing to address these issues through such a powerful medium. In the words of two audience members:

> I am at a loss for words... I just finished watching your documentary for the second time this morning ... Just wonderful. ... Congratulations! My expectations were high on all levels (content and use of media and editing) and you exceeded them on all counts. Just wonderful. (University professor, June, 2010)

> I liked your artistic shots and your summarising slides. I liked your approach to having different views integrated together – person on the street, educators, policy makers rather than divided into set groups – I can't believe you got access to all those people. (Audience member, June, 2010)

Inspired by the importance of what they see as a need to 'talk about these things', Nico and Amanda have also presented their documentary publically at education conferences and have started to design teaching units based on its key themes.

Therein lies for me the key reason why I will continue to assign multimodal identity texts as part of my teacher preparation classes. These projects not only get future teachers to experience directly the potential of this innovative pedagogy but they also create a much needed space for a future generation of teachers to join theory and practice and share with others their thoughts on the forces that will shape their classes to come.

References

Garcia, E, Arias, MB, Harris Murri, NJ, and Serna, C (2010) Developing responsive teachers: A challenge for a demographic reality. *Journal of Teacher Education* 61(1-2) p132-142

Gunderson, L (2007) *English-only instruction and immigrant students in secondary schools: A critical examination.* Mahwah, NJ: Lawrence Erlbaum Associates

Jacquet, M (2007) La formation des maîtres à la pluriethnicité: pédagogie critique, silence et désespoir. *Revue des sciences de l'éducation* 33(1) p25-45

Moldoveanu, M and Mujawamariya, D (2007) L'éducation multiculturelle dans la formation initiale des enseignants: Des politiques aux pratiques [Multicultural education in the initial training of teachers: From policies to practices]. *McGill Journal of Education* 42(1) p31-46.

Moore, D and Gajo, L (2009) Introduction-French voices on plurilingualism and pluriculturalism: Theory, significance and perspectives. *International Journal of Multilingualism* 6(2) p137-153

Further reading/viewing

Séror, J, Hennessey, A, and Paluzzi, N (2010, April) 'Are we multicultural?' Reflections on learning to teach in multicultural contexts. Paper presented at the CCERBAL Conference 2010, Ottawa. http://screencast.com/t/yZfYbL3ppD

Jérémie Séror website: http://www.ilob.uottawa.ca/fr/seror.php

Link to version of documentary http://www.arewe.ca

Case Study 18
Developing American Sign Language (ASL) Identity Texts
Kristin Snoddon

Introduction

This chapter summarises an exploratory study at the Ernest C. Drury School for the Deaf in Milton, Ontario, Canada. The study was part of the Multi-literacies Project. The format and objectives of the Multiliteracies Project were adapted to feature the Ontario ASL curriculum for first-language users as the basis of this study. The ASL curriculum is intended to foster ASL literacy across all grade levels at the three bilingual (ASL and English) provincial schools for Deaf students in Ontario. Through the production of ASL identity texts by grades 2, 3 and 5 students (approximately 7 to 10 years of age), this study focused on the cultivation of students' ASL identities and ASL literacy abilities.

Context

Academic learning of ASL, as supported by the Ontario ASL curriculum, is arguably the most powerful tool for activating prior knowledge, cognitive engagement and identity investment on the part of Deaf students. Since 1998, a team of Deaf teachers from three provincial schools have developed and field-tested this language arts curriculum. Overall expectations are in place for each grade relating to students' use of ASL grammar, ASL text and litera-ture construction and analysis, ASL media arts, and technology. In addition, the ASL curriculum's focus on supporting Deaf students' identities by incor-porating their language, culture and experience in course content makes it a vehicle for empowering education.

Process

An important feature of the Ernest C. Drury project was the involvement of visitors from the Deaf community. When inviting ASL storytellers to their classrooms, the teachers involved with this project chose individual Deaf adults who could expose students to classic Ontario ASL. This is the dialect of ASL used by students at the former Ontario School for the Deaf in Belleville. This dialect has largely been lost or displaced, especially among younger generations of Deaf Ontarians who often lack exposure to adult ASL models. These Deaf adult storytellers could also convey a sense of the heritage handed down from one Deaf generation to the next.

The Ernest C. Drury project focused on students' creation of ASL stories relating to traditional facets of Deaf culture and identity: name signs, life in residence, and sports. Over a three-week period, observations were made of individual classrooms and recorded via video camera and field notes. During the first week, the ASL storytellers visited each classroom. Their visits were recorded on the school's cameras and reviewed on monitors by teachers and students on the following days. During the second week, identity texts were created by students and shared with the rest of their class. The videos of the students' stories were then reviewed and edited. The final versions of these identity texts were then presented to the class.

Output

The students' development of ASL identity texts involved making multiple drafts, which were recorded and reviewed on video. For the grade 5 students, identity text development became a more sophisticated exercise than it was for younger students. Initially, the grade 5 students all tried to copy one adult storyteller's bold tone in their stories about ice skating and hockey. Guided by their teacher, however, the students were invited to compare different stories and then exercise their skills in literary criticism. As the students first watched a new story told by their teacher and then reviewed it on video, they were asked what needed improving and what details were missing from his narrative. The grade 5 teacher then retold his story by incorporating the students' suggestions, and the students remarked that his revised story was much more comprehensible. In this way, the students were inspired to create more individual identity texts and to provide each other with suggestions for improving their subsequent drafts. This episode highlighted the ASL curriculum's expectations for grade 5 students to be familiar with the ASL storytelling process and be able to produce and retell ASL texts in a variety of forms. Additionally, with their own identity texts, the students produced ASL stories which incorporated an introduction, event description, closing statement, and rich detail.

The grade 3 students also adopted one adult storyteller's bold attitude in their stories about sports. In this class some differences between the generations became apparent in students' telling of their sports stories. For the adult storytellers, sports were played at the residential schools with other Deaf students. When asked by their teachers what they had in common with the storytellers, the grade 3 students all mentioned sports. However, in their own stories, the students talked about playing outside school on teams with hearing children. These stories revealed the students' secure sense of their identities as Deaf athletes among hearing peers.

The grade 2 students narrated their personal histories of going to school and learning the name signs of their teachers and classmates. In contrast to the group-orientated discussion and instruction of the other classes, the grade 2 teacher guided her students individually through the storytelling process by reviewing each student's first draft on video and encouraging them to provide more detail about their experiences. Most of the grade two stories followed the same format, except for two students who came from hearing families. One of these students narrated his experiences of attending a mainstream school with no access to ASL. Among all the others, this story stands out as a powerful image of a student articulating his experience of disempowerment. This expressly documented self-reflection and self-analysis by a younger student demonstrates this project's success in promoting identity awareness and investment, and the collaborative critical inquiry that is fostered when Deaf students are encouraged to express their experiences and identities.

Impact

The enthusiasm and interest the students displayed for the storytellers are a reminder to educators that Deaf adults' presence in the classroom can be invaluable. These adults can serve as first-language models and share their life experiences and histories as Deaf people. They can also inspire the production of students' own ASL literature. In this way, the Ernest C. Drury project promotes the utilisation of the Deaf community, which is typically excluded from the classroom, as an educational resource.

The students' creation of identity texts revealed them to be confident, articulate storytellers in their own right. In their stories and during teacher-facilitated discussions, they were shown to be capable of discerning and analysing past and present inequities in their social environment.

Deaf students are no different from any other group of minority language students who are at risk of academic failure: just like many minority language groups, they too have experienced inappropriate categorisation and lack of accommodation by the school system. That the language and culture of the Deaf community are not routinely included in the standard curriculum for Deaf students reflects this systemic bias. This project highlights some ways in which identity promotion and investment can be incorporated into a bilingual bicultural education for Deaf students.

Further Reading

Snoddon, K (2010) Technology as a learning tool for ASL literacy. *Sign Language Studies*, 10(2), p197-213.

Websites

http://www.multiliteracies.ca/index.php/folio/viewProject/99 (Due to concerns about protecting students' identities, the ASL identity texts are not shown directly on the multiliteracies site).

The website of the Deaf Culture Centre in Toronto, Canada (www.deafculturecentre.ca) presents many identity texts (eg. poetry, stories etc.) that are accessible in four languages (ASL, langue des signes quebecoise [LSQ], English and French).

5

'It really comes down to the teachers, I think': Pedagogies of choice in multilingual classrooms

Jim Cummins, Margaret Early,
Lisa Leoni and Saskia Stille

Tomer's reflection on the impact one teacher made on his life (Chapter 3) highlights the power of instruction to expand students' learning opportunities and identity options. It also highlights the fusion of academic engagement and identity negotiation in the flow of classroom interactions orchestrated by the teacher. This process is illustrated in all the case studies described. These accounts of pedagogical practice, implemented in highly diverse locales, demonstrate that regardless of top-down policies and mandates that may be operating in different contexts, the teacher remains a powerful agent of change in the classroom. This is not to underestimate the challenges many teachers face. But each teacher's choice, big or small, implicit or explicit, can and does make an enormous difference in their students' lives.

Also evident in the pedagogical approaches described in the case studies is the considerable returns on investment, not only for the students themselves but also for the broader school and social communities. Topics and subject-matter knowledge that were previously invisible and inaccessible were made available for knowledge mobilisation in critical, democratic conversations across race, gender, age and class boundaries. Similarly, the affordances of multiple modes of meaning-making and the mediation of various digital tools enabled learners who had previously been silenced and often consigned to classroom activities well below their intellectual capacities to represent and communicate their knowledge at a more cognitively powerful level, thereby contributing to the collective intellectual capital of their communities. Thus, the pedagogical innovations linked to identity text work undertaken by the teachers produced highly engaged learning without vast amounts of one-size-fits-all pre-programmed resources being poured into the school or drip fed to the learner. Rather, the teachers respectfully and imaginatively honed, harnessed and redeployed the readily available rich resources within students and their communities, resources that are all too frequently squandered. In doing so, teachers enabled each learner to excel in specific ways.

We believe strongly that consideration of issues related to teacher-student identity negotiation is central to discussions of school effectiveness, particularly for schools serving socially marginalised communities. We are not alone in this conviction. As we have noted, there is a large body of empirical evidence, primarily from the fields of anthropology and sociology, that highlights the role of identity negotiation in student engagement and academic achievement. Unfortunately, this body of evidence is routinely ignored by policy-makers, with the result that issues related to teacher and student identities rarely find expression in school improvement plans or in top-down mandates. Not surprisingly from our perspective, these initiatives rarely bear fruit in raising attainment or in closing the achievement gap between social groups. For example, the Bush administration's *Reading First* initiative in the US, which was focused primarily on phonological awareness and phonics instruction, reported no improvement in students' reading comprehension or reading engagement among students in grades 1, 2, or 3 (Gamse *et al*, 2008).

One notable exception to this tendency to ignore identity issues in educational policy is the series of documents published by the Department for Education and Skills (DES) (2006) in the UK, as part of the Primary National Strategy. For example, the document *Excellence and Enjoyment: learning and teaching for bilingual children in the primary years. Unit 3. Creating an inclusive culture* highlighted the importance of developing a sense of belonging among students. The document notes that a sense of belonging is promoted when:

- children's ethnic, linguistic, cultural, religious and social backgrounds are included and reflected positively across the curriculum
- there are staff in school from the child's own background
- teachers model values and behaviour which promote equality and justice

■ the racism that is endemic in society is acknowledged; racist behaviour is recognised when it occurs, the damage it can do is appreciated and appropriate action is taken to prevent it

■ parents, carers and families from minority communities are acknowledged as key partners and empowered to play a role in their children's education. (p.9)

In this concluding chapter, we reflect on what school administrators and
teachers *can* do, both individually and collectively, to promote this sense of
belonging and a culture of accomplishment among students from marginalised social groups. We also sketch some linkages and extensions with respect
to how identity text work can be conceptualised within the broader fields of
language and literacy development. Specifically, we use the work of Michael
Halliday (1989) to map the spheres within which identity text work has taken
place thus far and also the range of language and literacy landscapes where
this work might be productively pursued.

Pedagogies of choice

Planned change in educational systems always involves *choice*. All of the
identity text projects described in this book are the result of choices made by
individual educators or groups of educators. Thus the first step for educators
interested in pursuing this pedagogical direction is to articulate and reflect
critically on the instructional choices that we make on a routine daily basis
and to examine alternative possibilities.

Administrators make choices at a broad system level, school principals make
choices at the level of individual schools, and teachers make choices within
their classrooms. At each level of decision-making, choices are constrained by
the realities of politically-imposed curriculum and assessment policies, funding, teacher availability and expertise in particular curricular areas, as well as
by student and community characteristics such as poverty, knowledge of the
language of instruction, etc. However, within the limitations imposed by
these realities, there are always degrees of freedom that permit educators to
make pedagogical choices that are not wholly constrained from the outside.
Even when educators do not consciously frame their instructional actions as
choices, they have nevertheless chosen these instructional actions (eg to
simply teach directly from the textbook) from among possible alternatives
that they may not have consciously articulated. Paradoxically, choice is not an
option – we have no choice but to choose from a range of instructional alternatives.

Thus individual educators always exercise agency – they are never powerless, although they frequently work in conditions that are oppressive both for them and for their students. While they rarely have complete freedom, educators do have choices in the way they structure the interactions in their classrooms. They determine for themselves the social and educational goals they want to achieve with their students. There are always options with respect to how educators orient their practice to students' language and culture, to the forms of parent and community participation they encourage, and to the ways they implement pedagogy and assessment. Educators therefore have the potential, individually and collectively, to work towards the creation of contexts of empowerment. Within these interpersonal spaces where identities are negotiated, students and educators can together generate power that challenges structures of inequity in small but significant ways.

It is worth emphasising that teacher identity is also directly implicated in the pedagogical choices they make. As educators, we are constantly sketching a triangular set of images:

- an image of our own identities as educators
- an image of the identity options we highlight for our students
- an image of the society we hope our students will help form.

Lisa recalls an experience which illustrates the fact that teacher identity is very much invested in the identity texts that their students create:

> I remember one day sitting in my room (at the end of second term) gazing at all the classroom walls filled with student identity texts. At that moment, I observed my teaching philosophy and pedagogical commitments come to life. I learned that every student expressed their identities in different ways and I was especially reminded that my instructional decisions mattered to them.

Lisa also points out that the choices teachers make about how they display and showcase students' identity text work sends important messages to students from marginalised communities:

> A teacher's decision to physically place student-produced narratives/identity texts (eg about the history of their countries) next to commercially-produced social studies or history textbooks sends a message to students that all histories displayed have equal validity and represent equal sources of knowledge. *Our classrooms are one big text!* Students – as early as preschoolers – *read* the walls of the classroom (and the school).

Identity texts also enable marginalised students to 'talk back' and re-position themselves in relation to racist or undermining societal discourses. In Lisa's words:

> I remember post 9/11, students would barge in to my class infuriated with the media coverage on Muslims. They would bring in newspaper clippings and even sometimes wrote quotes in their agenda books about what they had heard on CNN (one documentary in particular, *Beneath the Veil*, generated a lot of anger). So what's a teacher to do in this situation? Ignore student comments and feelings and start the math lesson on page 17? *Or* does the teacher use this time as an opportunity for students to talk, write, draw, speak about what they wish to express?
>
> For classrooms committed to critical literacy and transformative pedagogy, publishing identity texts represents a public testament – or a protest – since students are able to produce counter-narratives that speak out against the messages that portray them negatively.

Lisa's reflections on her own practice express clearly the extent to which teacher identity is infused with the process of identity text creation. Teachers' pedagogical commitments enable students' identity texts to reshape curriculum knowledge. In some cases, teachers' creation of their own identity texts acts as a catalyst for breaking the monopoly of dominant group control of knowledge production and identity positioning (see Ada and Campoy, 2004, and López-Gopar, this volume). Identity texts (re)position learners (and teachers) as active participants in the knowledge production that takes place in the classroom.

Administrators have a crucial role to play in establishing a school culture that invites transformative pedagogical approaches. Because of the increasing emphasis in many countries on accountability as measured by test scores, teachers may need reassurance from administrators that identity text work is legitimate and not dismissed as just 'off-task' behaviour. In turn, government policies, such as the Primary National Strategy (2006) document on creating an inclusive school culture, help open up spaces for both administrators and teachers to pursue pedagogical commitments that reflect their own identities and aspirations as educators.

Mapping future identity text work

The social practices the identity text authors engaged in cluster around three broad social functions:

- taking part in academic knowledge construction
- taking part in artistic and creative activities such as poetry and script writing, and
- social action linked to community life, such as the HIV/AIDS awareness activities in Uganda.

Halliday's (1989) distinctions between what he calls *field, tenor,* and *mode,* are helpful in thinking about aspects of the text in different social contexts. *Field* refers to the nature of the social activity taking place, including the topic or content; *tenor* refers to the nature of the roles and relationships between those taking part (eg a writer and her audience); and *mode* refers to both rhetorical features of the communication (eg narrative, persuasive, expository and so on) and the channel, which can be linguistic (spoken, written, or signed), visual, auditory, gestural, spatial or multimodal.

When we consider the identity texts discussed in previous chapters through this lens, we see that while some texts were aural and gestural, such as the wonderful poem performed by Penina Nafuye in Norton's vignette, most of the identity texts produced were in the written and visual *mode* (page and screen). Moreover, the rhetorical mode or genre most commonly employed was some form of narrative (eg retellings of myths, fairytales, legends, recounts of experiences and fictional stories).

With respect to *tenor* – the roles and relationships which were set up in the identity texts – the producers of these artefacts took on the discourse roles of expert informers, persuaders and narrators. In these roles, the students of all ages and proficiency levels presented 'identities of competence' (Manyak, 2004) that were realised and evidenced in their discourse. Unlike traditional patterns of social interaction between marginalised school students and their teachers, which tend to be hierarchical, the tenor of these texts is much closer to a relationship of mutual respect, in which power and social distance have been significantly reduced.

Regarding the *field* – the topics or content covered – the specifics of these ranged across sites and individual learners but, as we noted, there are a few commonalities in the texts produced. If we think of content varying along a continuum in the degree of technicality that has at one end (say the left end) everyday language and at the other end (the right) highly specialised technical language of specific fields and disciplines, most of the texts produced would be situated on the left to middle of the continuum. In other words, few authors of identity texts employed highly technical or specialised language. Additionally, most of the identity texts were about topics that related to the students' personal, home and community knowledge and interests – which were, in turn, shared to enrich the learning of their classmates and wider audience for whom this was new information. This is not surprising in view of teachers' desire to tap into and enable expression of students' experiences and cultural knowledge.

So, following these cursory observations across the cases, what might be helpful in thinking about where we go to develop the concept further in future? The range of practices could be extended in each of the inter-connected social practices in which learners engaged. They were clustered around academic knowledge generation, creative and artistic activities, and social action/community related activities. In the academic contexts, the activities were generally related to language arts and the humanities. Social practices and activities related to the sciences, mathematics and commerce are important areas in which to extend identity text creation in future. In the arts, poetry, play writing/directing, dance and quilt making occurred but extension to other modes, singular and combined, such as hip-hop, slam poetry, spatial design, film and musical compositions are also areas for development in the future. While most cases were connected to the community, since they were published online for a public audience, only a few of the projects described in this volume have had community activism as their primary function (although other projects within the Multiliteracies Project did have this focus – see www.multiliteracies.ca).

In our current project, *Engaging Literacies*, issues of inclusion and social justice have emerged in more focused ways. In some cases, the project provoked encounters with the social realities the children are dealing with – bullying, war and conflict, making new friends, moving to a new country. Many of the grade 3 and 4 students with whom we are working have come from war zones or have experienced natural disasters. These issues are allowed expression in the classroom because of the democratic nature of knowledge production in the creation of identity texts. Students as much as their teachers define the topics and set the agenda. When these issues have been raised in the context of our work together, we have made a deliberate choice to engage with them. It is not just issues like war and conflict that are complex. Controversial topics in the classroom and issues of language, culture and migration are equally complex when we look beneath the surface and explore with students their larger social significance.

Thus there is considerable scope for identity text work to engage with, and take action in pursuit of social justice (see also Marshall and Toohey, 2010).

Within the context of the Literacy Expertise framework (Figure 2.3), this increased focus on social justice work (together with the extensions of academic registers and artistic modes employed) would fall within the sphere of Focus on Use. For additional examples of identity text work oriented to social justice see http://www.nextgenerationpress.org/.

Moving to the Focus on Language dimension of the Literacy Expertise framework, we would envisage future collaborative work encompassing a broader range of fields or content areas beyond the humanities. Each specialised content area has its own disciplinary register, such as the particular language of mathematical problems, explanations of scientific phenomena, and information reports in geography, business studies and career and personal planning. Expanding identity text construction to a wider range of content-specific registers and genres would entail designing classroom practices that would move the learners along the field/content continuum to use more highly specialised and abstract linguistic forms and, along the tenor continuum, to more formal and distant discourse structures, while still maintaining the sense of pride, deep engagement and confidence we observed among identity text authors.

Future work could fruitfully pay greater *explicit* attention to teaching for transfer across languages and across modes. In several of the case studies reported here, there has been much talk among students about specific features of text and L1-L2 transfer. This could be considerably enhanced through explicit promotion of teachers' and students' critical language awareness of registers, genres, grammatical structures and cohesive devices in specific academic and social contexts. Additionally, it would be useful to encourage talk about language transfer that addresses the full range of transfer that is going on, such as conceptual, specific linguistic forms and functions, metacognitive and metalinguistic strategies, pragmatic aspects, and phonological and phonographemic dimensions. These sorts of conversations can also yield rich information about the place and function of different languages in students' lives and in their imagined futures, as well as in the lives of their parents and their communities.

With respect to the Focus on Meaning in the Literacy Expertise framework, there are many opportunities to explore the affordances, potentials and limitations of multiple modes in creating meaning and communicating to multiple audiences across different cultural worlds. As digital technologies expand and become increasingly accessible, the range of modes and their potential for interaction and infusion with each other will provide possibilities for identity text creation that we can barely imagine now. It is evident to us all that our communities, and the ways in which we communicate, are changing rapidly. Community is no longer geographically determined (as illustrated by Facebook and other forms of electronic communication). Communities that *are* geographically located are being transformed by the accelerated transnational flows of people.

These changes in communities and technologies have profound implications for how meanings are communicated and negotiated between authors and audiences. The pluralised notion of multiliteracies, together with the fusion of identity and literacy that identity texts represent, creates classroom and community spaces within which students and teachers can negotiate a broader range of text types and modes of communication, including written or digital text, images, sounds, video, performance/kinaesthetic, non-alphabetic literacies, and the multimodal combination of these.

The development of pedagogical approaches that enable students from marginalised social groups to develop critical literacy and become protagonists of their own emerging histories (Ada and Campoy, 2004) through identity text creation takes on new urgency in this rapidly changing social and educational context. It is no exaggeration to say that the future of humanity and of our planet depends on the extent to which upcoming generations develop the critical literacy skills to assess the validity of competing claims to knowledge. Whether it entails the portrayal of global issues and histories, or scientific debates such as the denial of evolution and climate change by many conservative groups, particularly in the US, dialogue and collaborative inquiry across multiple linguistic, cultural and national boundaries are key to resolving conflict and pursuing coherent solutions.

As noted by Jewitt (2008), the ways in which knowledge is represented and the modes through which it is communicated shape both what is to be learned and how it is to be learned. Critical literacy skills are essential to enabling learners to understand the affordances of different text types, and the ways in which language, discourse and modes of representation contribute to what a text means and how it is to be interpreted. To enable learners to engage deeply with their own and other perspectives in texts (broadly defined), educators need to draw students' attention to how knowledge is positioned, produced and represented. Students also need to be given multiple opportunities in a wide range of modalities to position, produce and represent their own knowledge and experiences. If they are not, they remain passive consumers of other people's knowledge and subject to the power relations that are embedded invisibly within this knowledge.

The core insight underlying identity text work is this: under current social and global conditions, education can lay claim to 'effectiveness' only when class-rooms become sites for knowledge production and teachers and students to-gether take on the roles of agents who are collaboratively producing this knowledge. The ways in which we author our stories, and produce and share knowledge will undoubtedly change rapidly in the coming years. However, we believe that the deep structure of identity text creation and its pedagogical power will remain much as described by the students and educators who have contributed to this volume.

Conclusion

In sum, this final chapter looks back at what has been accomplished and forward with renewed energy to what's next. Although many of the case studies described in this volume are inspirational, they do not represent any radical new vision of pedagogy. On the contrary, they are in the mainstream of what progressive educators – from John Dewey to Célestin Freinet to Paulo Freire – have advocated for generations. The core elements involve:

- linking curricular content to students' experience and identities
- fostering critical literacy skills along with critical awareness of how language works and is used for various social purposes
- enabling students to become active generators of knowledge and to express and expand their identities through various forms of cultural production
- promoting a social consciousness among students that values equa-lity, social justice and democratic participation.

Sadly, these approaches to pedagogy are in many contexts still outside the mainstream of what is actually happening in schools, particularly those which serve students from lower-income and marginalised groups. However, we believe that these new times afford unprecedented opportunities for change. It is in this spirit of knowledge mobilisation that we have compiled the case studies in this book.

The digital innovations that have transformed patterns of contact and com-munication over the past twenty years not only facilitate the production of identity texts but also enable students and teachers to communicate their work and insights to a global audience. The power of identity text work in promoting student engagement can be appreciated much more readily when it is presented electronically through multiple modalities (eg print, video, images, etc) and from multiple perspectives (eg testimonials from students, teachers and parents) than when it sits inert on a printed page. Thus, this work can be more readily and forcefully brought to the attention of policy-makers and those responsible for substantial institutional change than in the past. In the best case scenario, policy-makers will take heed and facilitate real change in educational structures. However, the change process is not dependent on the decisions of policy-makers; educators, individually and collectively, also exercise choice and their choices can transform the lives of students. Thus identity text work undertaken by teachers can represent a challenge to top-down mandates that are largely evidence-free, as is the case in many in educational jurisdictions around the world.

The case studies in this volume all illustrate the notion of *empowerment* – the collaborative creation of power. Across multiple geographical, social and educational landscapes, we have seen how power can be generated in the interactions of teachers and students. We hope that these case studies, shared among educators in widely diverse contexts, will also contribute to the collaborative creation of power and identity affirmation among educators themselves.

References

Ada, A F and Campoy, I (2004) *Authors in the Classroom: a transformative education process.* New York: Pearson/Allyn and Bacon

Ahrens, R, Annandale, K, Early, M, Fraser, A, Short, D and Tarlington, C (1978) *Bringing Unity into Language Development: Report 4 (A series of monographs).* Vancouver, BC: Vancouver School Board Publications

Althusser, L (1981) *On Ideology.* London: Verso.

August. D and Shanahan, T (eds) (2006) *Developing literacy in second-language learners. Report of the National Literacy Panel on Language Minority Children and Youth.* Mahwah, NJ: Erlbaum

August. D and Shanahan, T (eds) (2008) *Developing reading and writing in second-language learners. Report of the National Literacy Panel on Language Minority Children and Youth.* New York: Routledge

Bakhtin, MM (1986) *Speech genres and other late essays.* Austin: University of Texas Press

Bankston, C L and Zhou, M. (1995) Effects of minority-language literacy on the academic achievement of Vietnamese youths in New Orleans. *Sociology of Education*, 68, p1-17

Barnes, D. (1976) *From communication to curriculum.* Harmondsworth: Penguin

Bernhard, J K, *et al* (2006) Identity texts and literacy development among preschool English Language Learners: enhancing learning opportunities for children at risk of learning disabilities. *Teachers College Record,* 108(11), p2380-2405

Bernhard, J K, Winsler, A and Bleiker, C (2004) *The Early Authors Program: a Miami-Dade early literacy initiative.* Final report submitted to the Child Care Bureau's Early Learning Opportunities Office

Bishop, R and Berryman, M (2006) *Culture speaks: Cultural relationships and classroom learning.* Wellington: Huia Publishers, Aotearoa/New Zealand

Blommaert, J (2010) *The Sociolinguistics of Globalization.* New York: Cambridge University Press

Blommaert, J, Collins, J and Slembrouck, S (2005) Spaces of multilingualism. *Language and Communication*, 25(3) p197-216

Bransford, J D, Brown, A L and Cocking, R R (2000) *How people learn: Brain, mind, experience and school.* Washington, DC: National Academy Press

Browne, E (2002) *Handa's Hens.* London, England: Walker Books

Busch, B Jardine, A and Tjoutuku, A (2006) *Language biographies for multilingual learning* (Vol. 24). Cape Town: PRAESA Occasional Papers

Canagarajah, A S (2006) Toward a writing pedagogy of shuttling between languages: Learning from multilingual writers. *College English* 68(6). Retrieved November 12 2010 from www.outreach. psu.edu/programs/rsa/files/toward_a_writing_pedagogy_of_multilingual_writing.pdf

City of Toronto: Diversity. Retrieved August 12, 2010 from: http://www.toronto.ca/quality_of_life/diversity.htm

Chow, P and Cummins, J (2003) Valuing multilingual and multicultural approaches to learning. In SR Schecter and J Cummins (eds) *Multilingual Education in Practice: using diversity as a resource.* Portsmouth, NH: Heinemann

Clemente, A, Crawford, T, Garcia, L, Higgins, M, Kissinger, D, Lengeling, M M, Lopez Gopar, M, Narvaez, O, Sayer, P, and Sughrua, W (2006) A call for a critical perspective on English teaching in Mexico. *MEXTESOL Journal Special Issue: Critical Pedagogies*, 30(2), p13-17

Clemente, A and Higgins, M (2008) *Performing English with a Postcolonial Accent: ethnographic narratives from Mexico.* London: Tufnell Press

Clemente, A and Higgins, M (2010) 'Prison break': La praxis de las performancias lingüísticas en la prisión estatal de Oaxaca, México. Conferencia presentada en el *Encuentro Académico sobre Prácticas Culturales en el Lenguaje Oral y Escrito*, Universidad Autónoma 'Benito Juárez' de Oaxaca, Oaxaca, México, Enero 2010

Clemente, A and Higgins, M (2010, forthcoming) Performing methodological activities in post-colonial ethnographic encounters: Examples from Oaxaca, México. In F Shamim and R Qureshi (eds) *Perils, pitfalls and reflexivity in qualitative research in education.* Oxford: Oxford University Press

Clemente, A, Higgins, M and Sughrua, W (2010) 'Thanks for the blanket that was lent to me the first night': Ethnographic encounters with cultural practices of literacy in the state prison of Oaxaca. Paper submitted to *Journal of Language and Education*

Codó, E and Patiño, A (2010) Language choice, agency and belonging at a multilingual school in Catalonia. Paper presented at Sociolinguistics Symposium 18, University of Southampton, UK

Conteh, J Martin, P and Robertson, LH (eds) (2007) *Multilingual Learning Stories for Schools and Communities in Britain.* Stoke-on-Trent: Trentham Books

Corona, V Tusón, A and Unamuno, V (2008) Falar el nosotros de allá y el de ellos de aquí: a varia-cion do castelán como obxecto de reflexion e de ensino. In MT Diaz García, I Mas Alvarez and L Zas Varela (eds). *Integración Lingüística e Inmigración.* Santiago: Lalia-Universidade de Santiago de Compostela

Cook, V (1992) Evidence for multicompetence. *Language Learning*, 42, p557–591

Cook, V (1999) Going beyond the native speaker in language teaching. *TESOL Quarterly*, 33, p185–209

Cope, B and Kalantzis, M (eds) (2000) *Multiliteracies: literacy learning and the design of social futures.* New York: Routledge

Creese A and Blackledge, A (2010) Translanguaging in the bilingual classroom: A pedagogy for learning and teaching? *The Modern Language Journal* 94(1) p. 103-115

Cummins, J (1976) The influence of bilingualism on cognitive growth: A synthesis of research findings and explanatory hypotheses. *Working Papers on Bilingualism* 9 p1-43

Cummins, J (1979) Linguistic interdependence and the educational development of bilingual chil-dren. *Review of Educational Research* 49, p222-25l

Cummins, J (1981) Age on arrival and immigrant second language learning in Canada. A reassess-ment. *Applied Linguistics* 2, p l32-l49

Cummins, J (1996, 2001) *Negotiating Identities: education for empowerment in a diverse society.* Los Angeles: California Association for Bilingual Education

Cummins, J (1999) Alternative paradigms in bilingual education research: Does theory have a place? *Educational Researcher*, 28, p26-32

Cummins, J (2000) *Language, Power, and Pedagogy: bilingual children in the crossfire.* Clevedon: Multilingual Matters

Cummins, J (2004) Multiliteracies pedagogy and the role of identity texts. In K Leithwood, P McAdie, N Bascia and A. Rodigue (eds) *Teaching for Deep Understanding: towards the Ontario curriculum that we need.* Toronto: Ontario Institute for Studies in Education of the University of Toronto and the Elementary Federation of Teachers of Ontario

Cummins, J (2005) Teaching for cross-language transfer in dual language education: Possibilities and pitfalls. Paper presented at the TESOL Symposium on Dual Language Education: Teaching and Learning Two Languages in the EFL Setting, Bogazici University

Istanbul, Turkey. Retrieved November 12 2010 from www.achievementseminars.com/seminar_series_2005_2006/readings/tesol.turkey.pdf

Cummins, J (2006) Identity texts: The imaginative construction of self through multiliteracies pedagogy. In O Garcia, T Skutnabb-Kangas and ME Torres Guzman (eds.), *Imagining Multilingual Schools: languages in education and glocalization.* Clevedon: Multilingual Matters.

Cummins, J. (2007) Pedagogies for the poor? Re-aligning reading instruction for low-income students with scientifically based reading research. *Educational Researcher,* 36, p564–572.

Cummins, J, Chow, P and Schecter S (2006) Community as curriculum. *Language Arts* 83(4) p297-307

Cummins, J, Bismilla, V, Chow, P, Cohen, S, Giampapa, F, Leoni, L, Sandhu, P and Sastri, P (2005) Affirming identity in multilingual classrooms. *Educational Leadership,* 63(1), p38-43

Cummins, J, Bismilla, V, Cohen, S, Giampapa, F and Leoni, L (2005) Timelines and lifelines: Rethinking literacy instruction in multilingual classrooms. *Orbit* 36(1) p22-26

Cummins, J, *et al* (2006) ELL Students Speak for Themselves: Identity Texts and Literacy Engagement in Multilingual Classrooms. Retrieved November 18, 2010 from http://www.curriculum.org/secretariat/files/ELLidentityTexts.pdf

Department for Education and Skills (DES) (2006) *Excellence and Enjoyment: learning and teaching for bilingual children in the primary years. Unit 3. Creating an inclusive culture.* Primary National Strategy. London: DES

Dewey, J. (1916) *Experience and education.* New York: Collier Books.

Diaz Soto, L and Swadener, BB (eds) (2005) *Power and Voice in Research with Children.* New York: Peter Lang

Domínguez, C (2005) Towards a literary dialogue across borders. In A Selee (ed.), *Perceptions and Misconceptions in U.S.-Mexico Relations.* Washington D.C.: Woodrow Wilson International Center for Scholars, Mexico Institute, in collaboration with Letras Libres.

Doughty, P, Pearce, J and Thornton, G (1971) *Language in Use,* London: Edward Arnold (London Schools Council Programme in Linguistics and English Teaching)

Dru (2008) 'Seasons' [song]. On *The One* [album]

Dussel, E (2002) World-system and 'trans'-modernity. *Nepantla: Views from South* 3(2) p221-244

Early, M (1992a) Language and Content Learning K-12; The Vancouver School Board Project *Cross Currents: An International Journal of Language Teaching and Cross-Cultural Communication.* 58(2) p179-183

Early, M (1992b) Aspects of becoming an academically successful ESL student. In B Burnaby and A Cumming (eds) *Socio-political Aspects of ESL in Canada.* Toronto: OISE Press

Early, M (2008) Second and foreign language education in Canada. In NV Deusen-Scholl and NH Hornberger (eds) *Encyclopedia of Language and Education* (2nd ed., Vol. 4). Boston: Springer

Early, M and Gunderson, L (1993) Linking home, school and community language learning. *TESL Canada Journal* 11(1) p99-111

Early, M and Hooper, H. (1987) *Integrated language and content: A framework for teaching and learning.* Vancouver, BC: Vancouver School Board Publication.

Early, M and Hooper, H (2001) Implementation of the Vancouver School Board Initiatives. In B Mohan, C Leung and C Davison. *English as a Second Language in the Mainstream: teaching, learning, identity.* London: Pearson Longman

Early, M and Gunderson, L (1993) Linking home, school and community language learning. *TESL Canada Journal.* 11(1) p 99-111

Early, M, Thew, C and Wakefield, P (1986) *Integrating Language and Content Instructions K-12: An ESL Resource Book.* Victoria, BC: Queen's Printer

Early, M and Yeung, C (2009) Producing multimodal picture books and dramatic performances in core French: An exploratory case study. *Canadian Modern Language Review,* 66(2), p299–223

École Inuglak. (1999) *Un Inukshuk solitaire.* Markham, ON: Festival du Livre

Edwards, V (1998) *The Power of Babel: teaching and learning in multilingual classrooms.* Stoke-on-Trent: Trentham Books

Francis, N and Ryan, PM (1998) English as an international language of prestige: Conflicting cultural perspectives and shifting ethnolinguistic loyalties. *Anthropology and Education Quarterly,* 29(1), p25-43

Freire, P. (1970) *Pedagogy of the Oppressed.* New York: Continuum

Gallagher, E (2008) *Equal Rights to the Curriculum: many languages, one message.* Clevedon: Multilingual Matters

GallantxD2 (June 15, 2009) *Gr. 8 Portfolio, 2008-2009* [video]. Retrieved November 18, 2009, from http://www.youtube.com/user/GallantxD2#p/a/DA77D5061842CF0A/0/E5QWgq3MCSg

Gamse, BC *et al* (2008) *Reading First Impact Study: Final Report.* Washington DC: Institute for Educational Sciences

Garcia, E, Arias, MB, Harris Murri, NJ and Serna, C (2010) Developing responsive teachers: A challenge for a demographic reality. *Journal of Teacher Education* 61(1-2) p132-142

Gee, JP (2004) *Situated Language and Learning: a critique of traditional schooling.* London: Routledge

Gérin-Lajoie, D (2003) *Parcours identitaires de jeunes francophones en milieu minoritaire.* Sudbury: Les Éditions Prise de parole

Gibbons, P (2002) *Scaffolding Language, Scaffolding Learning: teaching second language learners in the mainstream classroom.* Portsmouth, NH: Heinemann

Giampapa, F (2010) Multiliteracies, pedagogy and identities: teacher and student voices from a Toronto elementary school'. *Canadian Journal of Education,* 33(2) p407-431

Gibney, M and Skogly, S (2010) *Universal Human Rights and Extraterritorial Obligations.* Philadelphia: University of Pennsylvania Press

Globe and Mail (2005) Suburbs suffer inner-city ills, but little relief offered: report pA4. Retrieved May 14, 2005, from http://www.globeandmail.ca

Goldberg, M (2006) *Integrating the Arts: an approach to teaching and learning in multicultural and multilingual settings* (3rd ed). Boston: Pearson Allyn and Bacon

Goodman, S (2006) Literature and technology. In S Goodman and K O'Halloran (eds) *The Art of English: literary creativity.* New York: Palgrave MacMillan

Gunderson, L (2007) *English-only Instruction and Immigrant Students in Secondary Schools: a critical examination.* Mahwah, NJ: Lawrence Erlbaum Associates

Guthrie, J T (2004) Teaching for literacy engagement. *Journal of Literacy Research,* 36 p1-30

Halliday, MAK (1985/1989) Part A. In M. A. K. Halliday and R. Hasan, *Language, context and text: Aspects of language in a social semiotic perspective*. Geelong, VIC/Oxford: Deakin University Press/Oxford University Press.

Halliday, MAK (1986/2007) Language across culture. In J J Webster (ed) *Language and Education, Volume 9 in the Collected Works of M.A.K. Halliday*. New York: Continuum

Halliday, MAK (1996) Literacy and linguistics: a functional perspective. In R Hasan and G Williams (eds) *Literacy in Society*. London: Longman

Higgins, C and Norton, B (eds) (2010) *Applied linguistics and HIV/AIDS*. Bristol, UK: Multilingual Matters

Holland, D, Lachicotte, W, Skinner, D and Cain C (1998) *Identity and Agency in Cultural Worlds*. Cambridge, MA: Harvard University Press.

Issa T and Williams, C (2009) *Realising Potential: complementary schools in the UK*. Stoke-on-Trent: Trentham Books

INALI. (2008) *Catálogos de lenguas indígenas nacionales*. Retrieved September 8, 2008, from http://www.inali.gob.mx/catalogo2007/

Jacquet, M (2007) La formation des maîtres à la pluriethnicité: pédagogie critique, silence et désespoir. *Revue des sciences de l'éducation* 33(1) p25-45

Jewitt, C (2008) Multimodality and literacy in school classrooms. *Review of Research in Education*, 32, p241-267.

Kamler, B. (2001) *Relocating the Personal: a critical writing pedagogy*. New York: State University of New York Press

Kanno, Y and Norton, B (2003) Imagined communities and educational opportunities: Introduction. *Journal of Language, Identity, and Education* 2(4) p241-249

Kenner, C (2000) *Home Pages: literacy links for bilingual children*. Stoke-on-Trent: Trentham Books

Kendrick, M and Jones, S (2008) Girls' visual representations of literacy in a rural Ugandan community. *Canadian Journal of Education*, 31(2), p371-404

Kendrick, M Jones, S Mutonyi, H and Norton, B (2006) Multimodality and English education in Ugandan schools. *English Studies in Africa*, 49(1) p95-114

Kendrick, M and McKay, R (2004) Drawings as an alternative way of understanding young children's constructions of literacy. *Journal of Early Childhood Literacy*, 4, p109-128

Knowles, JG and Cole, AL (eds) (2008) *Handbook of the ARTS in Qualitative Research: perspectives, methodologies, examples and issues*. London: Sage Publications

Kourtis-Kazoullis, V (2001) DiaLogos: bilingualism and the teaching of second languages on the Internet. Rhodes: University of the Aegean, Unpublished doctoral dissertation

Kourtis-Kazoullis, V and Tzanetopoulou, A (2003) *We, the Others: studying diversity in the social environment of the school*. Rhodes, Greece: University of the Aegean [in Greek].

Kourtis-Kazoullis,V Papantonakis, G, Makrogianni, T and Kladogenis, D-I (2009) An Internet-based learning environment for the teaching of Greek as a second language through literary texts: Theory and practice. In E Close, G Couvalis, G Frazis, M Malaktsoglou and Tsianikas M (eds.) Greek Research in Australia: Proceedings of the Biennial International Conference of Greek Studies, Flinders University June 2007. Flinders University Department of Languages – Modern Greek: Adelaide. Retrieved November 12 2010 from http://dspace.flinders.edu.au:8080/dspace/bitstream/2328/8085/1/321-334_Kourtis-Kazoullis%20et%20al.pdf

Kress, G and van Leeuwen, T (2006) *Reading Images: the grammar of visual design (2nd ed)*. New York: Routledge

Ladson-Billings, GJ (1995) Toward a theory of culturally relevant pedagogy. *American Education Research Journal*, 35 p465-491

Lam, SE (2000) L2 Literacy and design of the self: A case study of a teenager's writing on the internet. *TESOL Quarterly* 40 p.183-20

Lavoie, C (2008a) 'Hey, Teacher, Speak Black Please': The educational effectiveness of bilingual education in Burkina Faso. *The International Journal of Bilingual Education and Bilingualism* 12(1), p1-17

Lavoie, C (2008b) Developing multiliteracies through bilingual education in Burkina Faso. *Educational Research and Review*, 3(11), p344-350

Liang, X (1999) Dilemmas of cooperative learning: Chinese students' experiences. Unpublished doctoral dissertation. University of British Columbia, Vancouver, BC

Lindsay, J (2010) *Children's Access to Print Material and Education-related Outcomes: findings from a meta-analytic review.* Naperville, IL: Learning Point Associates

López-Gopar, ME (2009) 'What makes children different is what makes them better': Teaching Mexican children 'English' to foster multilingual, multiliteracies, and intercultural practices. Unpublished Doctoral Dissertation, University of Toronto, Toronto, Canada

López -Gopar, ME, Clemente, A and Sughrua, W (in press) Co-creating identities through identity texts and dialogical ethnography. *Writing and Pedagogy*

López -Gopar, ME, Stakhnevich, J, León García, H and Morales Santiago, A (2006) Teacher educators and pre-service English teachers creating and sharing power through critical dialogue in a multilingual setting. *MEXTESOL Journal Special Issue: Critical Pedagogies*, 30(2), p83-104

Lotherington, H and Chow, S (2006) Rewriting 'Goldilocks' in the urban, multicultural elementary school. *The Reading Teacher* 60(3) p244-252

Mackay, D, Thompson, B and Scaub, P (1970) *Breakthrough to Literacy: teachers' manual.* London: Longman (London Schools Council Programme in Linguistics and English Teaching)

Man, E. and Lim, J. (2003) Promoting use of the Internet in English language teaching. *Journal of Basic Education*, 12(2) p156-174

Manyak, PC (2004) 'What did she say?' Translation in a primary-grade English immersion class. *Multicultural Perspectives* 6, p12-18

Marshall, E and Toohey, K (2010) Representing family: Community funds of knowledge, bilingualism, and multimodality. *Harvard Educational Review*, 80(2), p221-241

McCarty, T L (ed) (2005) *Language, Literacy, and Power in Schooling.* Mahwah, NJ: Lawrence Erlbaum Associates.

McKinney, C. and Norton, B. (2008) Identity in language and literacy education. In B Spolsky, and F Hult (eds) *The Handbook of Educational Linguistics.* London: Blackwell.

Mignolo, W (2001) Colonialidad del poder y subalternidad. In I. Rodriquez (ed) *Convergencia de Tiempos: estudios subalterno/contextos latinoamericanos: Estado, cultura, subalternidad.* Amsterdam and Atlanta: Editions Rodopi B.V.

Mills, L A (1991) *The Rag Coat.* New York: Little Brown Books for Young Readers

Mohan, B (1986) *Language and Content.* Reading, MA: Addison-Wesley

Mohan, B (2001) The second language as a medium of learning. In B Mohan, C Leung and C Davison (eds) *English as a Second Language in the Mainstream: teaching, learning, identity.* London: Pearson Longman

Moje, E B and Luke, A (2009) Literacy and identity: Examining the metaphors in history and contemporary research. *Reading Research Quarterly* 44(4) p415-437

Moldoveanu, M and Mujawamariya, D (2007) L'éducation multiculturelle dans la formation initiale des enseignants: Des politiques aux pratiques [Multicultural education in the initial training of teachers: From policies to practices]. *McGill Journal of Education* 42(1) p31-46

Moore, D and Gajo, L (2009) Introduction–French voices on plurilingualism and pluriculturalism: Theory, significance and perspectives. *International Journal of Multilingualism* 6(2) p137-153

Mushengyezi, A (2003) Rethinking indigenous media: Rituals, 'talking' drums and orality as forms of public communication in Uganda. *Journal of African Cultural Studies* 16 p107-128

Mutonyi, H (2005) The influence of pre-conceptual and perceptual understandings of HIV/AIDS: A case study of selected Ugandan biology classrooms M.A. thesis, University of British Columbia

Naqvi, R (2008) Opening doors to literacy in Canada's multicultural classrooms: an introduction to dual language books research and the database project. Retrieved December 15, 2010 from http://www.rahatnaqvi.ca/files/poster.pdf

National Reading Panel (2000) *Teaching Children to Read: an evidence-based assessment of the scientific research literature on reading and its implications for reading instruction.* Washington, DC: National Institute of Child Health and Human Development

New London Group (1996, 2000) A pedagogy of multiliteracies: Designing social futures. *Harvard Educational Review,* 66, 60-92. Reprinted in B. Cope and M. Kalantzis (eds) *Multiliteracies: Literacy learning and design of social futures.* London: Routledge

Newman, D, Griffin, P. and Cole, M. (1989) *The Construction Zone.* Cambridge: Cambridge University Press

Norton, B (2000) *Identity and Language Learning: gender, ethnicity and educational change.* Harlow: Longman/Pearson Education

Norton, B (2010) Language and identity. In NH Hornberger and SL McKay (eds) *Sociolinguistics and Language Education.* Bristol: Multilingual Matters

Norton, B (in press) Investment. *Routledge Encyclopedia of Second Language Acquisition.* London and New York: Routledge

Norton, B and Mutonyi, H (2007) Talk what others think you can't talk: HIV/AIDS clubs as peer education in Ugandan schools. *Compare: Journal of Comparative Education,* 37(4), 479-492.

Ock, S and Han, J (April 6, 2009) *Never Change* [song and video]. Retrieved December 11, 2009 from http://www.youtube.com/watch?v=462GNf0nl4c

Organisation for Economic Cooperation and Development. (2004) *Messages from PISA 2000.* Paris: Author.

Omoniyi, T (2003) Local Policies and Global Forces: multiliteracy and Africa's Indigenous languages. *Language Policy,* 2, p133-152

Pavlenko A and Blackledge A (eds) (2004) *Negotiation of Identities in Multilingual Contexts.* Clevedon: Multilingual Matters

Pennycook, A (2007) ELT and colonialism. In J Cummins and C Davison (eds.) *International Handbook of English Language Teaching* (Volume 1). New York: Springer

Pennycook, A (2010) Nationalism, identity, and popular culture. In N. Hornberger and S. McKay (eds). *Sociolinguistics and language education,* Bristol: Multilingual Matters.

Portes, A and Rumbaut, RG (2001) *Legacies: The Story of Immigrant Second Generation.* Berkley: University of California Press

Purcell-Gates, V (2007) Complicating the complex. In V. Purcell-Gates (ed) *Cultural Practices of Literacy: case studies of language, literacy, social practice, and power.* Mahwah, New Jersey: Lawrence Erlbaum Associates, Inc.

Purcell-Gates, V (2008) Real-life Literacy Instruction, K-3: Handbook for Teachers. The Cultural Practice of Literacy Study, UBC. Available at http://www.authenticliteracyinstruction.com/

Rowsell, J and Pahl, K (2007) Sedimented identities in texts: Instances of practice. *Reading Research Quarterly* 42(3) p388-404

Schechter, S and Cummins, J (eds) (2003) *Multilingual Education in Practice: using diversity as a resource*. Portsmouth, NH: Heinemann

Skourtou, E, Kourtis-Kazoullis, V and Cummins, J (2006) Designing virtual learning environments for academic language development. In J Weiss, J Nolan, J Hunsinger and P Trifonas (eds) *The International Handbook of Virtual Learning Environments*. Dordrecht: Springer

Skutnabb-Kangas, T (1984) *Bilingualism or Not: the education of minoritites*. Clevedon, England: Multilingual Matters

Skutnabb-Kangas, T (2000) *Linguistic Genocide – or worldwide diversity and human rights*. Mahwah, NJ: Lawrence Erlbaum Associates

Smucker, B (1995) *Selina and the Bearpaw Quilt*. Toronto: Lester Publishing

Sneddon, R (2009) *Bilingual Books, Biliterate Children: learning to read through dual language books*. Stoke-on-Trent: Trentham Books

Snoddon, K. (2010) Technology as a learning tool for ASL literacy. *Sign Language Studies*, 10(2), p197-213

Snow, C E, Burns, M S, and Griffin, P (eds.) (1998) *Preventing Reading Difficulties in Young Children*. Washington, DC: National Academy Press.

Stein, P. (2008) *Multimodal pedagogies in diverse classrooms: Representation, rights and re-sources*. London and New York: Routledge.

Stein P and Newfeld D (2003) Recovering the future: Multimodal pedagogies and the making of culture in South African classrooms. *International Journal of Learning*, 10 2841-2850

Unamuno, V. (2009) Dinàmiques sociolingüístiques i immigració: l'escola com a microcomunitat. In C. Junyent *et al* (ed). *Llengua i acollida*. Barcelona: Horsori

United Nations AIDS (UNAIDS, 2004) *Life-skills-based HIV/AIDS education in schools*. Available on line at: http://www.unaids.org/ungass/en/global/UNGASS19_en.htm (accessed November 11, 2004)

Vygotsky, L S (1978) *Mind in society: The development of higher social processes*. Cambridge, MA: Harvard University Press.

Wohlwend, KE (2009) Damsels in discourse: Girls consuming and producing identity texts through Disney princess play. *Reading Research Quarterly*, 44(1) p57-83

Index